P9-DGS-183

PACIFIC CREST TRAIL
Data Book

Mileages, landmarks, facilities,
resupply data, and essential trail information
for the entire Pacific Crest Trail,
from Mexico to Canada

WILDERNESS PRESS ... *on the trail since 1967*

North Cascades
Manning Park
Skykomish
Stehekin
Seattle
Snoqualmie Pass
Washington
Mt. Rainier NP
Mt. St. Helens
White Pass
Portland
Cascade Locks
Mt. Hood
Olallie Lake
Oregon
Cascade Summit
Crater Lake NP
Ashland
Hyatt Lake
Seiad Valley
Mt. Shasta
Castella
Burney Falls State Park
Old Station
Lassen Volcanic NP
Belden
Sierra City
Echo Lake
Lake Tahoe
Reds Meadow
Edison Lake
Bishop
Independence
Kings Canyon NP
Lone Pine
Sequoia NP
Mt. Whitney
California
Kennedy Meadows
Tehachapi
Mojave
Lancaster
Dulce
Big Bear City
Los Angeles
Idyllwild
Warner Springs

千里の みちも いっぽから。

The Journey of a Thousand Ri begins with the first step.

Pacific Crest Trail Data Book

5th EDITION 2013
   4th printing 2016

Copyright © 1997, 2000, 2001, 2005, 2013 by Benedict Go and Wilderness Press

ISBN 978-0-89997-745-4; eISBN 978-0-89997-746-1

Manufactured in the United States of America

Published by: **Wilderness Press**
 c/o AdventureKEEN
 2204 First Avenue South, Suite 102
 Birmingham, AL 35233
 (800) 443-7227; fax (205) 326-1012
 info@wildernesspress.com
 www.wildernesspress.com

Regional section maps are used with permission of Andrew Alfred-Duggan.

Thanks to the following photographers for contributing their lively images:

Page vi: *(top left and bottom right)* Pacific Crest Trail Association/Heather Tilert, *(top right)* Pacific Crest Trail Association/Ron Kelley, *(middle right)* Audrey Alfred-Duggan, *(bottom left)* Pacific Crest Trail Association/Caitlin Barale, *(middle left)* Pacific Crest Trail Association/Deems Burton

Page 129: *(top left and top right)* Paul Gerald, *(bottom right)* Pacific Crest Trail Association/Joe Walters, *(bottom left)* Pacific Crest Trail Association/Don Saviers, *(middle left)* Pacific Crest Trail Association/Caitlin Barale

NOTICE: The author and publisher caution users of the data contained herein that land and resource managers along the route of the PCT can, and often do, make changes to the trail's routing, thereby changing or invalidating the information. Post Offices and resupply points may be closed for numerous reasons at any time, so verify mailing addresses before shipping supplies. While every attempt has been made to verify this data as this book goes to print, contact the Pacific Crest Trail Association (PCTA) and local agencies for current conditions and recent changes.

ACKNOWLEDGMENTS

I would like to thank Wilderness Press and the authors of the PCT guidebooks, especially Jeff Schaffer, for permitting the use of the guidebooks as the basis for the creation of the Data Book. Thank you also to the PCTA for all they do for the trail, Ray Jardine for publishing his ideas on long-distance hiking, Cindy Ross for sharing her journal, Matt Maxon for re-measuring much of the Southern California section mileages, various trail users and maintainers who provided feedback on this book, and to Ada Leung for production assistance on this book. Send any changes or comments to Ben: **thork_erin@yahoo.com.**

FROM THE AUTHOR: THE JOURNEY

The future begins with a dream . . . . And what a wonderful dream it was! I thru-hiked the Pacific Crest Trail in 1996; to this day, memories of that life continue to make me smile. The sweet innocence of the unknown, the lessons still to be learned. How I yearn to feel those moments! I started on the PCT not fully knowing what to expect. It was the most challenging journey I had ever attempted.

The long expanse of the desert, the refreshing High Sierra, and the beautiful Cascade Mountains—nature became my home. Every night, I slept in different places, sometimes on a hill, in a valley, or on top of a mountain. I found myself seeking and finding special places, and treasuring the times when I could feel deeply. In nature, I saw more moments that in my mind could not be possible, and yet they happened. I remember the uncertainty, the not knowing of what would be. But, at the same time, as my knowledge increased and gave power, it also limited me. Knowledge created a boundary that at times became the border of my life. It was only by questioning what I knew and in doing difficult things that I could grow. Here I learned my four treasured lessons:

Take care of those whom you love.
Take care of your health.
Do not limit yourself to what you know. Try and learn.
Share your life. We are not meant to be alone.

I am glad that many continue to protect this most beautiful treasure.
To the future!

—Ben "Gentle Ben" Go, June 2013

A note about my trail name: When I started on the PCT, I met many Appalachian Trail thru-hikers, most of whom had trail names. For two months, I hiked across Southern California with the veteran AT hikers pondering what my trail name should be. We finally reached Kennedy Meadows and saw the movie *Grizzly Adams*. Next thing I knew, my trail name Gentle Ben came into being, bestowed by the one and only "Rude Dog."

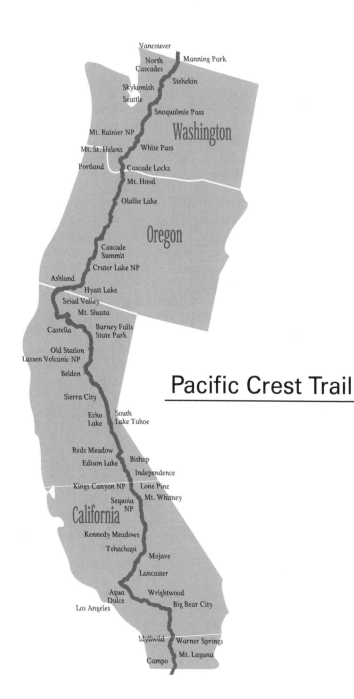

Vancouver
North Cascades
Manning Park
Stehekin
Skykomish
Seattle
Snoqualmie Pass
Mt. Rainier NP
Washington
Mt. St. Helens
White Pass
Portland
Cascade Locks
Mt. Hood
Olallie Lake
Oregon
Cascade Summit
Crater Lake NP
Ashland
Hyatt Lake
Seiad Valley
Mt. Shasta
Castella
Burney Falls State Park
Old Station
Lassen Volcanic NP
Belden
Sierra City
Echo Lake
South Lake Tahoe
Reds Meadow
Edison Lake
Bishop
Independence
Kings Canyon NP
Lone Pine
Sequoia NP
Mt. Whitney
California
Kennedy Meadows
Tehachapi
Mojave
Lancaster
Agua Dulce
Wrightwood
Los Angeles
Big Bear City
Idyllwild
Warner Springs
Mt. Laguna
Campo

Pacific Crest Trail

CONTENTS

On the Trail

Introduction

The *Pacific Crest Trail Data Book* contains a summary of the entire Pacific Crest Trail (PCT), covering a distance of more than 2,660 miles from Mexico to Canada. The trail passes through three states: California, Oregon, and Washington. The PCT terrain varies from desert in Southern California, to the mountains of the High Sierra in Central California, to the Cascades in far Northern California and continuing through Oregon and Washington.

This book was created as an adjunct to Wilderness Press's PCT guidebooks for planning, tracking, and as a quick reference on the trail. Trail information is comprised of landmarks, listed as they occur in a northerly direction, from Mexico to Canada. For each landmark, the following information is given: the mileage between points; the mileage from the Mexican border; its elevation; available facilities (such as water sources and post offices); and an occasional water alert when the next water source is more than 12 miles away.

This book provides:

- An easy calculation of distances between any two points on the trail.
- A profile of the trail elevation changes.
- Assistance in preparing for hiking sections of the trail or the entire trail (a "thru hike").
- Assistance in establishing daily mileage goals while on the trail.
- The average angle of the trail in degrees between the previous landmark and the current landmark.

Information in this 5th edition was obtained using the 2003 editions of the *PCT Southern California* and *Northern California* guidebooks and the 2004 edition of the *Oregon & Washington* guidebook. It also includes updates and comments from various trail users, maintainers, and government agencies. It is not intended for use as a navigation tool, nor does it provide any description of the trail's environment. For more information about the trail, including topographic strip maps, consult the three PCT guidebooks. The books are available from the PCTA, various outdoor equipment stores, or Wilderness Press.

Pacific Crest Trail Association
1331 Garden Highway
Sacramento, CA 95833
(916) 285-1846
www.pcta.org

Wilderness Press
PO Box 43673
Birmingham, AL 35243
(800) 443-7227
www.wildernesspress.com

California Snow Depth Measurements

The following table contains snow depths at various points in California, measured around April 1st of each year. The value 0.0 is used when data is not available. For an indication of the location of these various points:

- Bighorn Plateau is next to Mt. Whitney, the highest point in the 48 contiguous states.
- Bishop Pass is at a junction between Mather Pass and Muir Pass.
- Piute Pass is at a junction just after Muir Pass.
- Tuolumne Meadows is in Yosemite National Park.
- Bond Pass is part of the Tahoe-Yosemite Trail next to the PCT.
- Deadman Creek is next to Sonora Pass.
- Upper Carson Pass is in the Lake Tahoe area.
- Lower Lassen Peak is by Lassen National Park.
- Shasta Region is around the Mt. Shasta area.

Beneath each heading is a course number, which refers to the snow course number assigned by the Department of Water Resources (DWR) in California. For the latest information on these points, contact DWR through their web page at **http://cdec.water.ca.gov/cgi-progs/snowQuery** and use the course numbers. Below the course numbers are the elevations for these points, then followed by the actual snow depths in inches starting with the year 1989. At the bottom of the table is an average of the snow depths at each point.

California Snow Depth Measurements

Year	Bighorn Plateau (C# 250)	Bishop Pass (C# 222)	Piute Pass (C# 183)	Tuolumne Meadows (C# 161)	Bond Pass (C# 159)
	11,350	11,200	11,300	8,600	9,300
1989	43.6	62.5	78.9	43.3	101.7
1990	23.7	43.9	56.8	26.8	61.5
1991	67.3	76.1	90.1	65.2	123.8
1992	37.3	52.3	62.8	33.5	65.7
1993	90.7	125	138	81.9	150
1994	41.1	62.6	70.5	33	68.5
1995	96.4	157.3	162.1	106.5	204.8
1996	70.1	94.6	111.4	61.6	116.2
1997	68.4	92	110.9	61.5	107.8
1998	99	133	132.7	92.4	147
1999	32.6	66.5	77.1	57.5	115.1
2000	56.1	71.7	80.1	43.4	104
2001	36.7	59.3	57.7	32	63.6
2002	65.3	79.7	78.7	55.3	108.9
2003	49.1	72.9	70.8	42.8	87.4
2004	41.1	61.5	77.4	39.9	78.5
2005	90.1	113.1	110	94	153.4
2006	53	130.1	124.2	98.1	162.1
2007	20	39.7	51.1	19.6	52.9
2008	65	72.8	85.3	48.7	91.6
2009	59.3	70.7	82	58.6	110
2010	62.5	81.5	94.6	54.1	92.6
2011	106	132.9	129	105	175.5
2012	20.6	45.6	49	29.4	58.1
2013	27	55.2	61	34	75.8
AVERAGE	56.9	82.1	89.7	56.7	107.1

California Snow Depth Measurements

Year	Deadman Creek (C# 345)	Carson Pass (C# 106)	Lassen Peak (C# 047)	Shasta Region (C# 018)
	9,250	8,500	8,250	7,900
1989	83.7	81.3	223	128.6
1990	50	49.1	106.4	75.9
1991	95.5	98.6	151.7	95
1992	56.1	52.3	127.7	102.7
1993	107.5	116.6	225.8	136.9
1994	47.8	39.3	101.3	73.9
1995	141.9	149.4	276.2	197.4
1996	87.9	88.8	171	112.8
1997	86.3	66.1	136	110.6
1998	117	112.2	250.3	196.5
1999	82.7	108.5	194.8	152
2000	75.3	69.8	178.4	139.4
2001	57.6	42	109.1	88.9
2002	73.6	78.3	166.3	113.1
2003	64.1	55	185.7	150.7
2004	57.2	50.1	187.1	138.1
2005	124.8	112	173.8	61.1
2006	137.3	123.4	266.5	0
2007	50.2	45.5	112.1	77.1
2008	69.9	57.1	132.5	82.4
2009	73.8	70	146.8	94.9
2010	70.3	74	169.5	144.3
2011	138.5	134.1	242.8	0
2012	43.1	53	145.1	120.6
2013	57	46.5	140.9	100.5
AVERAGE	82	78.9	172.8	117.1

California Snow Depth Measurements

Crossing the High Sierra

The High Sierra in California has always been the major barrier for doing a thru-hike of the PCT. If you intend to do a thru-hike, the following equation is provided as a simple way of estimating when to reach Kennedy Meadows, the beginning of the High Sierra, en route to crossing the Sierra. You will still encounter plenty of snow, but it should not be overwhelming.

Kennedy Meadows Day = June 1 + (snow depth at Bighorn Plateau divided by 3.5) days

Note that the snow depths at Bighorn Plateau for various years are provided two pages back. Using this equation, the Kennedy Meadows Days starting with 1998 are:

Year	Equation	Result
1998	June 1 + (99 / 3.5) days = June 1 + 29 days	June 30
1999	June 1 + (33 / 3.5) days = June 1 + 10 days	June 11
2000	June 1 + (56 / 3.5) days = June 1 + 16 days	June 17
2001	June 1 + (37 / 3.5) days = June 1 + 11 days	June 12
2002	June 1 + (65 / 3.5) days = June 1 + 19 days	June 20
2003	June 1 + (49 / 3.5) days = June 1 + 14 days	June 15
2004	June 1 + (41 / 3.5) days = June 1 + 12 days	June 13
2005	June 1 + (90 / 3.5) days = June 1 + 26 days	June 27
2006	June 1 + (53 / 3.5) days = June 1 + 15 days	June 16
2007	June 1 + (20 / 3.5) days = June 1 + 6 days	June 7
2008	June 1 + (65 / 3.5) days = June 1 + 19 days	June 20
2009	June 1 + (59 / 3.5) days = June 1 + 17 days	June 18
2010	June 1 + (63 / 3.5) days = June 1 + 18 days	June 19
2011	June 1 + (106 / 3.5) days = June 1 + 30 days	July 1
2012	June 1 + (21 / 3.5) days = June 1 + 6 days	June 7
2013	June 1 + (27 / 3.5) days = June 1 + 8 days	June 9

Heading and Code Definitions

The column headings and codes used in the Resupply and Trail Data sections follow. The example used in the explanation refers to the following entry:

Landmark	Facilities	Diff	S->N	Elev	Gra	Map
Highway 138	w,R	0.8	518.4	3040	-1.8	E10
Water Alert (↓): 16.4m						
Water Alert (↑): 30.7m						

LANDMARK

The Landmark column contains a brief description of the trail at this location. In the example above, the landmark is Highway 138.

FACILITIES

The Facility column contains codes corresponding to features available at this location. In the example above, "w" means that this location is a water source. The codes and their definitions follow:

Direction Codes

N   North, direction toward the North Pole

S   South, direction toward the South Pole

E   East, direction from which the sun rises

W   West, direction to which the sun sets

Combinations of these codes are also used to designate in-between directions, such as NW for Northwest or SE for Southeast.

Heading and Code Definitions

Facility Codes

PO   Post Office. Packages can be mailed to and from this office.

w   Water source. Depending on the season and time of year, a water source may not have water. Call the PCTA for information.

G   Groceries, stores, supermarkets

M   Meals, restaurants, deli

L   Lodging, hotels, motels

sh   Shower

r   Register

R   Road

m   Miles

,   Comma. Facilities separated by commas are in the same location. For example, "P.O.,w,G 0.30m N" means that the post office, water source, grocery are all located 0.3 mile North.

;   Semi-colons. Facilities separated by semi-colons are not all in the same location. For example, "w;G 0.30m SE;sh" means that the water source and shower are nearby while the grocery is 0.3 mile Southeast.

The facility column is also used to give alerts of distances of water sources. Depending on the season, water sources do dry up. The guidebooks contain more information on the dependability of these sources. Call the PCTA for the latest water conditions. The criterion for water alerts is when the next water source within half a mile of the trail is more than 12 miles away. In the example above, **Water Alert** (↓):16.4m means that the next nearby water source reading down (heading north toward Canada) is 16.4 miles away, while **Water Alert** (↑):30.7m means that the next nearby water source reading up (heading south toward Mexico) is 30.7 miles away. These mileages include the side trail distances from the PCT to the water source, accounting for the differences in mileage heading north or south.

Heading and Code Definitions

DIFF

The Difference column contains the mileage difference between the previous landmark to the current landmark. In the example above, 0.8 mile means that Highway 138 is 0.8 mile from the previous landmark, a jeep road.

S->N

The S->N column contains the miles using the PCT southern terminus at the Mexican border as mile 0.0 and heading north. The mileage is cumulative to allow easy computation of distances between any two points on the trail. In the example above, 518.4 means that Highway 138 is 518.4 miles from the southern terminus.

ELEV

The Elevation column refers to the approximate elevation of the landmark. In the example above, 3040 means that Highway 138 is at an elevation of 3,040 feet.

GRA

The Gradient column shows the average angle of the trail in degrees between the previous landmark to the current landmark. In the example on page 6, -1.8 means that the trail is going down at an average of 1.8 degrees from the jeep road to Highway 138. If the number is positive, then the trail is going up. A large positive or negative number indicates that that part of the trail is steep. As a general guideline, the PCT follows the "no more than 15 degrees going uphill and no less than 15 degrees going downhill" rule.

MAP

The Map column refers to the maps in the Wilderness Press PCT guidebooks for the landmarks. In the example above, E10 means that Highway 138 is located in the E10 map of the *Southern California* guidebook.

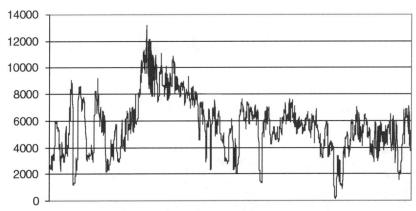

**Elevation Profile for Entire Pacific Crest Trail
from Mexico to Canada**

PCT Total Mileage: 2,666.1 miles

RESUPPLY DATA

Landmark	Facilities	Diff	S->N	Elev	Gra	Map
General Delivery Campo, CA 91906 (619) 478-5466	PO,w,G,r, R: 0.30m N	1.3	1.3	2600	-2.0	A1
General Delivery Mt. Laguna, CA 91948 (619) 473-8341	PO,w,G,M,L,r, R: 0.40m S	41.7	43.0	5980	0.2	A7
General Delivery Warner Springs, CA 92086 (760) 782-3166	PO,w,M,r, R: 1.20m NE	66.6	109.6	3040	-2.7	A14
Kamp-Anza RV Park Attn: (Your Name) PCT Hiker 41560 Terwilliger Road Space 19, Attn: PCT Anza, CA 92539 (951) 763-4819	w,G,sh,r, R: 5.80m NW	33.1	142.7	4075	-1.5	B5
General Delivery Anza, CA 92539 (951) 763-2074	PO,w,G,M,L,r, R: 7.00m W	8.6	151.3	4919	-3.3	B5
General Delivery Idyllwild, CA 92549 (951) 659-9719	PO,w,G,M,L,sh,r, R: 4.50m W	27.3	178.6	8100	-3.9	B9

RESUPPLY DATA

Landmark	Facilities	Diff	S->N	Elev	Gra	Map
General Delivery Cabazon, CA 92230 (951) 849-6233	PO,w,G,M,r, R: 4.50m W	31.0	209.6	1360	2.2	B11
General Delivery Big Bear City, CA 92314 (909) 585-7132	PO,w,G,M,L,r, R: 3.00m SE	64.5	274.1	7260	-1.9	C7
General Delivery Cedar Glen, CA 92321 (909) 337-4614	PO,w,G,M,L, R: 4.30m SW	23.1	297.2	4580	-1.6	C11
Best Western Inn Attn: (Your Name) PCT Hiker 8317 US Highway 138 Phelan, CA 92371 (760) 249-6777	w,G,M,L, R: 0.60m NW	44.9	342.1	3000	-1.2	C17
General Delivery Wrightwood, CA 92397 (760) 249-8882	PO,w,G,M,L, R: 4.50m N	21.5	363.6	8250	0.5	D3
General Delivery Acton, CA 93510 (661) 269-8618	PO,w,G,M, R: 5.80m E	80.6	444.2	2237	-4.0	D13
General Delivery Lake Hughes, CA 93532 (661) 724-9281	PO,w,G,M,L,sh, r,R: 2.20m NE	42.1	486.3	3050	-2.7	E6
Hikertown c/o Richard Skaggs Attn: (Your Name) PCT Hiker 26803 W. Avenue C-15 Lancaster, CA 93536 (661) 724-0086	w,G,sh,r, R: 0.10m NE	32.1	518.4	3040	-1.8	E10
General Delivery Tehachapi, CA 93581 (661) 822-0279	PO,w,G,M,L,r, R: 9.40m W	39.9	558.3	4150	2.7	E15
General Delivery Mojave, CA 93502 (661) 824-3502	PO,w,G,M,L,r, R: 12.00m E	0.0	558.3	4150	2.7	E15
General Delivery Onyx, CA 93255 (760) 378-2121	PO,w,G,r, R: 17.60m W	93.7	652.0	5246	2.6	F13

RESUPPLY DATA

Landmark	Facilities	Diff	S->N	Elev	Gra	Map
Kennedy Meadows General Store P.O. Box 3A-5 Inyokern, CA 93527	w,G,r,R: 0.70m SE	50.8	702.8	6020	0.2	G7
General Delivery Lone Pine, CA 93545 (760) 876-5681	PO,w,G,M,L,r, R: 24.90m E	42.0	744.8	10500	1.6	G12
General Delivery Independence, CA 93526 (760) 878-2210	PO,w,G,M,L,r, R: 24.00m E	45.4	790.2	10710	2.8	H4
Muir Trail Ranch Attn: (Your Name) PCT Hiker Box 176 Lakeshore, CA 93634-0176	w 1.50m NW;R	66.0	856.2	7890	-1.0	H13
Vermillion Valley Resort c/o Rancheria Garage Attn: (Your Name) PCT Hiker 62311 Huntington Lake Road Lakeshore, CA 93634 (559) 259-4000 Via UPS Only!	w,G,M,L, R: 6.00m W	21.0	877.2	7850	-5.0	H15
General Delivery Mammoth Lakes, CA 93546 (760) 934-2205	PO,w,G,M,L,r, R: 7.25m NE	25.6	902.8	8920	-0.9	H18
General Delivery Tuolumne Meadows, CA 95389 (209) 372-4475	PO,w,G,M,L,sh, r,R: 0.30m W	38.8	941.6	8690	0.6	H23
Lake of the Sky Outfitters Attn: (Your Name) PCT Hiker 1023 Emerald Bay Road South Lake Tahoe, CA 96150 (530) 541-1027 Open 7 days, call to check	w,G,M,L,sh,r, R: 9.50m NE	151.4	1093.0	7220	-2.6	J9
General Delivery South Lake Tahoe, CA 96150 (530) 541-4365	PO,w,G,M,L,sh, R: 9.70m NE	0.0	1093.0	7220	-2.6	J9
General Delivery Echo Lake, CA 95721 (530) 659-7207	PO,w,G,M,L,r,R	1.5	1094.5	7414	-6.0	J9

RESUPPLY DATA

Landmark	Facilities	Diff	S->N	Elev	Gra	Map
General Delivery Tahoe City, CA 96145 (530) 583-6563	PO,w,G,M,L, R:12.00m NE	32.3	1126.8	7650	2.4	K5
General Delivery Soda Springs, CA 95728 (530) 426-3082	PO,w,G,M,r, R: 3.20m W	29.0	1155.8	7090	1.6	K8
General Delivery Sierra City, CA 96125 (530) 862-1152	PO,w,G,M,L,r, R: 1.50m SW	41.8	1197.6	4570	-0.8	M1
General Delivery Belden, CA 95915 (530) 533-8206	PO,w,r,R: 0.90m SW	91.7	1289.3	2330	2.2	M11
General Delivery Chester, CA 96020 (530) 258-4184	PO,w,G,M,L,sh, R: 8.00m NE	46.5	1335.8	4990	0.9	N7
General Delivery Old Station, CA 96071 (530) 335-7191	PO,w,G,M,L,sh, r,R: 0.30m N	41.9	1377.7	4580	-0.5	N12
General Delivery Cassel, CA 96016 (530) 335-3100	PO,w,G,r,R: 1.50m SW	34.0	1411.7	2990	-0.8	N18
General Delivery Burney, CA 96013 (530) 335-5430	PO,w,G,M,L, R: 7.00m SW	4.2	1415.9	3110	-1.8	N18
PCT Hikers Recreation Resource Mgmt Attn: (Your Name) PCT Hiker 24900 Highway 89 Burney, CA 96013 (530) 335-5713	w,G,M,sh,r, R: 0.10m E	7.7	1423.6	2950	-0.4	N19
General Delivery Castella, CA 96017 (530) 235-4413	PO,w,G,sh,r, R: 2.00m SW	82.2	1505.8	2180	-2.9	O11
General Delivery Dunsmuir, CA 96025 (530) 235-0338	PO,w,G,M,L, R: 4.50m N	0.7	1506.5	2130	-0.8	P1
General Delivery Etna, CA 96027 (530) 467-3981	PO,w,G,M,L,sh, R: 10.40m NE	99.8	1606.3	5960	-6.1	P14

RESUPPLY DATA

Landmark	Facilities	Diff	S->N	Elev	Gra	Map
General Delivery Seiad Valley, CA 96086 (530) 496-3211	PO,w,G,M,r,R	55.8	1662.1	1371	-0.6	Q9
General Delivery Ashland, OR 97520 (541) 552-1622	PO,w,G,M,L, R: 12.40m N	57.6	1719.7	6060	-2.7	R9
General Delivery Ashland, OR 97520 (541) 552-1622	PO,w,G,M,L, R: 12.90m N	6.9	1726.6	4240	-0.4	R10
Hyatt Lake Resort Attn: (Your Name) PCT Hiker 7900 Hyatt Prairie Road Ashland, OR 97520 (541) 482-3331 Via UPS only!	w,G,M,sh,r, R: 0.75m N	23.6	1750.2	5090	3.5	B5
General Delivery Crater Lake, OR 97604 (541) 594-3115	PO,w,G,M,L,r, R: 4.50m NE	80.2	1830.4	6108	-1.7	C10
Crater Lake Lodge Attn: (Your Name) PCT Hiker 565 Rim Drive Crater Lake, OR 97604 (541) 594-2255 x3200 Via UPS Only!	w,G,M,L, R: 2.80m SE	4.5	1834.9	7075	4.5	C10
General Delivery Crater Lake, OR 97604 (541) 594-3115	PO,w,G,M,L,r, R: 2.80m SE	0.0	1834.9	7075	4.5	C10
Shelter Cove Resort Attn: (Your Name) PCT Hiker West Odell Lake Road Highway 58 Crescent Lake, OR 97425 (541) 433-2548 Held for 2 weeks Via UPS Only!	PO,w,G,sh,r, R: 1.40m SE	77.3	1912.2	5003	-2.7	D13
Elk Lake Resort Attn: (Your Name) PCT Hiker 60000 Century Drive Bend, OR 97701 (541) 480-7378 Via UPS or FedEx Only! $5 handling fee	w,G,M,L,sh, R: 1.10m E	46.1	1958.3	5250	0.1	E7

RESUPPLY DATA

Landmark	Facilities	Diff	S->N	Elev	Gra	Map
Olallie Lake Resort c/o USFS Estacada Station Attn: (Your Name) PCT Hiker 595 NW Industrial Way Estacada, OR 97023	w,G,R: 0.10m E	94.8	2053.1	4950	-3.6	F7
General Delivery Government Camp, OR 97028 (503) 272-3238	PO,w,G, R: 6.00m W	49.3	2102.4	4155	-0.1	F14
Timberline Ski Area WY'East Store Attn: (Your Name) PCT Hiker 27500 East Timberline Road Timberline Lodge, OR 97028 (503) 272-3189 (503) 272-3129 $5 handling fee	w,G,M,L,r, R: 0.10m S	4.9	2107.3	5940	3.3	G1
General Delivery Cascade Locks, OR 97014 (541) 374-5026	PO,w,G,M,L,sh, r,R: 0.25m NE	46.1	2153.4	240	-4.8	G7
White Pass P.O. (The Kracker Barrel Store) Attn: (Your Name) PCT Hiker 48851 US Highway 12 Naches, WA 98937 (509) 672-3105	PO,w,G,M,sh,r, R: 0.70m W	147.8	2301.2	4405	-4.9	H19
Chevron Gas Station Attn: (Your Name) PCT Hiker 521 State Route 906 Snoqualmie Pass, WA 98068 (425) 434-6688	w,G,M,L, R: 0.20m SE	98.9	2400.1	3000	-1.1	I15
Summit Inn Attn: (Your Name) PCT Hiker 603 State Route 906 P.O. Box 163 Snoqualmie Pass, WA 98068 (425) 434-6300 $15 + tax if not staying	w,G,M,L,r, R: 0.20m SE	0.0	2400.1	3000	-1.1	I15
General Delivery Skykomish, WA 98288 (360) 677-2241	PO,w,G,M,L,r, R: 14.00m W	74.6	2474.7	4060	-5.7	J8
General Delivery Stehekin, WA 98852 (509) 682-2625	PO,w,G,M,L, sh,r,R: 10.60m E	102.0	2576.7	1600	-5.4	K14

ON THE TRAIL

Mile-by mile trail data,
including landmarks, facilities,
cumulative mileages, elevations,
and trail gradients

PCT Total Mileage: 2,663.5 miles

SOUTHERN CALIFORNIA

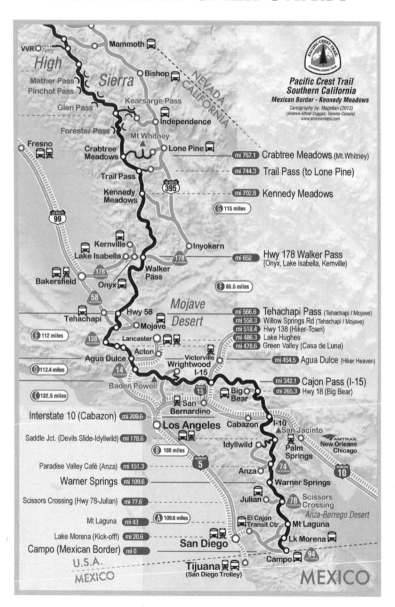

Pacific Crest Trail
Southern California
Mexican Border - Kennedy Meadows
Cartography by: Magellan (2013)
(Andrew Alfred-Duggan, Toronto-Canada)
www.andrewmaps.com

VVRO Ferry
Mammoth
High
Mather Pass
Pinchot Pass
Sierra
Bishop
NEVADA
CALIFORNIA
Glen Pass
Kearsarge Pass
Forester Pass
Independence
Fresno
Mt Whitney
Crabtree Meadows
Lone Pine
Crabtree Meadows (Mt.Whitney) — mi 767.1
Trail Pass
Trail Pass (to Lone Pine) — mi 744.3
Kennedy Meadows
Kennedy Meadows — mi 702.8
395
G 115 miles
99
Kernville
Inyokern
Lake Isabella
Hwy 178 Walker Pass — mi 652
(Onyx, Lake Isabella, Kernville)
Bakersfield
178
Walker Pass
Onyx
F 85.5 miles
58
Mojave Desert
Tehachapi
Hwy 58
Tehachapi Pass (Tehachapi / Mojave) — mi 566.6
Mojave
Willow Springs Rd (Tehachapi / Mojave) — mi 558.3
Hwy 138 (Hiker-Town) — mi 518.4
E 112 miles
138
Lancaster
Lake Hughes — mi 486.3
Acton
Green Valley (Casa de Luna) — mi 478.6
Agua Dulce
Victorville
Wrightwood
Agua Dulce (Hiker Heaven) — mi 454.5
14
I-15
D 112.4 miles
Baden Powell
Cajon Pass (I-15) — mi 342.1
Hwy 18 (Big Bear) — mi 265.3
15
Big Bear
San Bernardino
C 132.5 miles
Interstate 10 (Cabazon) — mi 209.6
Los Angeles
Cabazon
I-10
San Jacinto
AMTRAK
New Orleans
Chicago
Saddle Jct. (Devils Slide-Idyllwild) — mi 178.6
Idyllwild
Palm Springs
B 100 miles
10
Paradise Valley Café (Anza) — mi 151.3
5
Anza
74
Warner Springs — mi 109.6
Warner Springs
Scissors Crossing (Hwy 78-Julian) — mi 77.6
Julian
78
Scissors Crossing
Anza-Borrego Desert
Mt Laguna — mi 43
A 109.6 miles
El Cajon Transit Ctr.
Mt Laguna
Lake Morena (Kick-off!) — mi 20.6
Lk Morena
Campo (Mexican Border) — mi 0
San Diego
Campo
94
U.S.A.
MEXICO
Tijuana
(San Diego Trolley)
MEXICO

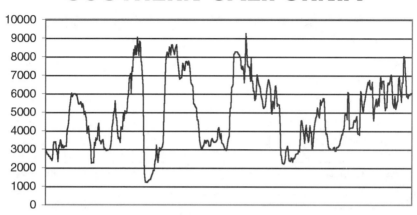

SOUTHERN CALIFORNIA

Elevation Profile for Southern California
From the Border to Kennedy Meadows

Section Total Mileage: 702.8 miles

Landmark	Facilities	Diff	S->N	Elev	Gra	Map
Mexican Border	—	0.0	0.0	2915	0.0	A1
San Diego Gas & Electric, cross a dirt road	R	0.3	0.3	2810	-3.8	A1
Cross another dirt road	R	0.3	0.6	2710	-3.6	A1
Cross Forrest Gate Road	R	0.1	0.7	2710	0.0	A1
Three old concrete steps next to Forrest Gate Road	R	0.6	1.3	2600	-2.0	A1
General Delivery Campo, CA 91906 (619) 478-5466	PO,w,G,r, R: 0.30m N	0.0	1.3	2600	-2.0	A1
PCT-posted crossing of Highway 94	—	1.0	2.3	2475	-1.4	A1
San Diego & Arizona Eastern Railroad's tracks	—	0.6	2.9	2475	0.0	A1
Creeklet, winter and early spring	w	1.4	4.3	2380	-0.7	A1
Reach poor jeep road	R	1.2	5.5	2550	1.5	A2

17

SOUTHERN CALIFORNIA

Landmark	Facilities	Diff	S->N	Elev	Gra	Map
Pipe gate to little used road	R	3.7	9.2	3350	2.3	A2
Another jeep road	R	0.2	9.4	3400	2.7	A2
Cross east-descending jeep road	R	1.9	11.3	3345	-0.3	A2
Viewpoint of Hauser Mountain	—	0.5	11.8	3400	1.2	A3
South Boundary Road 17S08	R	2.7	14.5	2910	-2.0	A3
Junction with a1988-vintage trail segment	—	0.8	15.3	2810	-1.4	A3
Cross Hauser Creek, winter and early spring	w	0.7	16.0	2320	-7.6	A3
Saddle southeast of Morena Butte	—	1.4	17.4	3210	6.9	A3
Leave jeep trail	—	0.2	17.6	3150	-3.3	A3
Viewpoint north over the southern Laguna Mountains	—	1.0	18.6	3495	3.7	A3
Jeep road in a saddle	R	0.3	18.9	3390	-3.8	A3
Corner of Lake Morena Drive and Lakeshore Drive	w;G 0.30m SE; sh;R	1.7	20.6	3065	-2.1	A3
Ridgetop	—	1.4	22.0	3220	1.2	A3
Bridge over Cottonwood Creek, winter and early spring	w	2.6	24.6	3065	-0.6	A5
Cottonwood Creek, winter and early spring	w	1.4	26.0	3105	0.3	A5
Boulder Oaks Campground	w	0.4	26.4	3170	1.8	A5
Boulder Oaks Road	R	0.1	26.5	3165	-0.5	A5
Grassy plain	w,G	0.3	26.8	3150	-0.5	A5
Kitchen Creek Road	R	3.8	30.6	3990	2.4	A5
Fred Canyon, creek usually dry	w	1.8	32.4	4205	1.3	A6
Fred Canyon Road 16S08	w,R: 0.80m NW	0.6	33.0	4410	3.7	A6
Long Canyon	w	4.0	37.0	5230	2.2	A6
Long Canyon Creek ford	w	1.1	38.1	5435	2.0	A6
Second road crossing	R	1.0	39.1	5900	5.1	A6
Morris Ranch Road	R	1.1	40.2	6005	1.0	A6

SOUTHERN CALIFORNIA

Landmark	Facilities	Diff	S->N	Elev	Gra	Map
Cross road next to La Posta Creek	R	0.7	40.9	5825	-2.8	A7
South Boundary of Burnt Rancheria Campground	—	0.7	41.6	5950	1.9	A7
Spur to Burnt Rancheria Campground	—	0.7	42.3	5970	0.3	A7
Paved road leading to Stephenson Peak	R	0.7	43.0	5980	0.2	A7
General Delivery Mt. Laguna, CA 91948 (619) 473-8341	PO,w,G,M, L,r,R: 0.40m S	0.0	43.0	5980	0.2	A7
Second paved road	R	0.6	43.6	5895	-1.5	A7
Saddle where some jeep roads terminate	R	1.9	45.5	5900	0.0	A7
Flathead Flats	—	0.9	46.4	5715	-2.2	A8
Dirt spur descending from highway, junction to Laguna/ El Prado Campground	w,sh,R: 0.20m SE	1.5	47.9	5440	-2.0	A8
Dirt road that descends to Oasis Spring	R	0.1	48.0	5430	-1.1	A8
G.A.T.R. Road, faucet southwest across Highway S1 at Penny Pines	w,R: 0.12m SW	0.9	48.9	5440	0.1	A8
Barren Saddle	R	0.5	49.4	5562	2.6	A8
Saddle west of Garnet Peak	—	1.6	51.0	5495	-0.5	A8
Pioneer Mail Trailhead Picnic Area, late spring and summer	w	1.7	52.7	5260	-1.5	A8
Water Alert (↓) 24.9m						
Kwaaymii Point Road	R	0.7	53.4	5450	2.9	A8
Jeep road down to Oriflamme Canyon	R	1.4	54.8	5250	-1.6	A8
Another jeep road down to Oriflamme Canyon	R	2.9	57.7	4875	-1.4	A9
Second ridgetop	R	1.3	59.0	5060	1.5	A9

SOUTHERN CALIFORNIA

Landmark	Facilities	Diff	S->N	Elev	Gra	Map
Faint jeep track above Oriflamme Canyon	w: 1.70m W	2.1	61.1	4770	-1.5	A9
Mason Valley Truck Trail	—	1.1	62.2	4690	-0.8	A10
Upper Chariot Canyon, by a road junction, water 0.6m through 1.8m N	w,R: 1.80m N	1.3	63.5	3860	-6.9	A10
Mason Valley cutoff road	R	0.3	63.8	4075	7.8	A10
Cross a gap	—	2.6	66.4	4240	0.7	A10
Cross Rodriguez Spur Truck Trail, water 0.9m through 1.3m W	w: 1.30m W	2.0	68.4	3650	-3.2	A10
Rocky gap on Granite Mountain's north ridge	—	3.2	71.6	3390	-0.9	A11
Another gap	—	1.9	73.5	3130	-1.5	A11
Reach Highway S2	R	2.9	76.4	2245	-3.3	A11
Cross Highway S2	R	0.8	77.2	2275	0.4	A11
Cattle gate next to concrete bridge, next to San Felipe Creek	—	0.2	77.4	2250	-1.4	A11
Cross Highway 78, San Felipe Creek, maybe contaminated	w,R	0.2	77.6	2252	0.1	A11
Water Alert (↓) 23.8m						
Water Alert (↑) 24.9m						
Pipe gate, pass the crest of San Felipe Hills	—	8.5	86.1	3360	1.4	A12
Dry, sandy wash	—	0.6	86.7	3210	-2.7	A12
Ridgecrest	—	1.6	88.3	3600	2.6	A12
Junction with an east-branching jeep road	R	2.1	90.4	3485	-0.6	A12
Poor jeep road beyond a pipe gate	R	0.8	91.2	3550	0.9	A12
Cattle gate	—	2.7	93.9	4155	2.4	A13
Veer northeast through a gap	—	1.9	95.8	4395	1.4	A13
Barrel Spring	w	5.6	101.4	3475	-1.8	A13
Water Alert (↑): 23.8m						

SOUTHERN CALIFORNIA

Landmark	Facilities	Diff	S->N	Elev	Gra	Map
Montezuma Valley Road S22	R	0.1	101.5	3445	-3.3	A13
PCT post marking the crossing of a jeep road	R	2.1	103.6	3285	-0.8	A13
San Ysidro Creek	w	1.6	105.2	3355	0.5	A13
Cross a good dirt road	R	1.1	106.3	3495	1.4	A14
Cross ridgetop jeep road	R	1.4	107.7	3510	0.1	A14
Bridge of 2-lane Highway 79	w,R: 0.20m NE	1.9	109.6	3040	-2.7	A14
General Delivery Warner Springs, CA 92086 (760) 782-3166	PO,w,M,r, R: 1.20m NE	0.0	109.6	3040	-2.7	A14
Recrossing jeep road	R	0.7	110.3	2960	-1.2	B1
Cross Aqua Caliente Creek, usually dry	—	0.6	110.9	2910	-0.9	B1
Privately operated campground	—	0.2	111.1	2925	0.8	B1
Bridge under Highway 79	R	0.3	111.4	2930	0.2	B1
Old jeep trail	—	0.6	112.0	2960	0.5	B1
Junction with a dirt road	R	0.2	112.2	2965	0.3	B1
Large campsite, end of dirt road	R	0.3	112.5	2975	0.4	B1
Aqua Caliente Creek	w	2.6	115.1	3195	0.9	B2
Switchback in a side canyon	—	1.0	116.1	3520	3.5	B2
Lost Valley Road	R	2.4	118.5	4170	2.9	B2
Spur road pass Lost Valley Road	w,R: 0.20m NW	1.0	119.5	4450	3.0	B2
Water Alert (↓): 17.4m						
Drop east to a saddle	—	3.0	122.5	4945	1.8	B2
Chihuahua Valley Road	R	4.6	127.1	5050	0.2	B3
Combs Peak	—	1.9	129.0	5595	3.1	B3
Tule Canyon	—	2.2	131.2	4710	-4.4	B3
Junction with old temporary PCT	—	0.9	132.1	4675	-0.4	B3
Dirt road at the Anza-Borrego Desert State Park boundary	R	2.1	134.2	4110	-2.9	B4

SOUTHERN CALIFORNIA

Landmark	Facilities	Diff	S->N	Elev	Gra	Map
Tule Canyon Creek	—	2.0	136.2	3590	-2.8	B4
Tule Canyon Road	w,R: 0.25m SE	0.4	136.6	3640	1.4	B4
	Water Alert (↑): 17.3m					
Coyote Canyon Road	R	2.7	139.3	3500	-0.6	B4
Nance Canyon seasonal creeklet, early spring	w	0.5	139.8	3350	-3.3	B4
	Water Alert (↓): 29.6m					
Chamise-covered gap	—	2.1	141.9	4185	4.3	B4
Sandy jeep road	R	0.8	142.7	4075	-1.5	B4
Kamp-Anza RV Park Attn: (Your Name) PCT Hiker 41560 Terwilliger Road Space 19, Attn: PCT Anza, CA 92539 (951) 763-4819	w,G,sh,r, R: 5.80m NW	0.0	142.7	4075	-1.5	B5
Table Mountain's shoulder	—	3.8	146.5	4910	2.4	B5
Alkali Wash	—	1.2	147.7	4540	-3.3	B5
Low pass across the flanks of Lookout Mountain	—	3.1	150.8	5070	1.9	B5
Pines-to-Palms Highway 74	w,M,R: 1.00m NW	0.5	151.3	4919	-3.3	B5
General Delivery Anza, CA 92539 (951) 763-2074	PO,w,G,M, L,r,R: 7.00m W	0.0	151.3	4919	-3.3	B5
Penrod Canyon Creek, usually dry	—	3.7	155.0	5040	0.4	B6
Road 6S01A	R	2.0	157.0	5700	3.6	B6
Saddle on Desert Divide, junction to Tunnel and Live Oak Springs	w: 1.00m E	1.0	158.0	5950	2.7	B6
Cross private mining road	—	1.4	159.4	6400	3.5	B6
Climbers trail to Lion Peak	—	0.7	160.1	6600	3.1	B6
Cedar Spring Trail 4E17, junction to Cedar Spring Camp	w: 1.00m N	2.2	162.3	6780	0.9	B7
Saddle with a junction to Morris Ranch	—	0.7	163.0	6945	2.6	B7

SOUTHERN CALIFORNIA

Landmark	Facilities	Diff	S->N	Elev	Gra	Map
Trail 4E04	—	0.4	163.4	7080	3.7	B7
Fobes Ranch Trail 4E02	—	2.9	166.3	5990	-4.1	B7
Apache Spring Trail	w: 0.50m E	2.6	168.9	7430	6.0	B7
Water Alert (↑): 29.1m						
Gap on San Jacinto's crest	—	2.9	171.8	7200	-0.9	B8
Above Andreas Canyon	—	3.4	175.2	8380	3.8	B9
Join Tahquitz Valley Trail	w: 0.33m N	1.5	176.7	8075	-2.2	B9
Tahquitz Peak Trail 3E08	—	0.6	177.3	8570	9.0	B9
Saddle Junction	—	1.3	178.6	8100	-3.9	B9
General Delivery Idyllwild, CA 92549 (951) 659-9719	PO,w,G,M,L, sh,r,R: 4.50m W	0.0	178.6	8100	-3.9	B9
Wellmans Cienaga Trail	—	1.9	180.5	9030	5.3	B9
Strawberry Cienaga	—	1.0	181.5	8560	-5.1	B9
Marion Ridge Trail 3E17	—	1.5	183.0	8070	-3.5	B9
North Fork San Jacinto River, below Deer Springs	w	1.9	184.9	8830	4.3	B10
Water Alert (↓): 20.7m						
Fuller Ridge	—	2.2	187.1	8725	-0.5	B10
Fuller Ridge Trailhead Remote Campsite	—	3.1	190.2	7750	-3.4	B10
Black Mountain Road 4S01	w,R: 1.30m SW	0.2	190.4	7670	-4.3	B10
Switchback in dirt road	R	1.9	192.3	6860	-4.6	B10
Narrow gap	—	1.3	193.6	6390	-3.9	B10
Falls Canyon & One Horse Ridge Overlook	—	2.3	195.9	5372	-4.8	B10
View of Fuller Ridge	—	2.4	198.3	4385	-4.5	B10
Small saddle west of knob 3252	—	3.2	201.5	3200	-4.0	B10
Snow Canyon Road, water out of a fountain	w,R	4.1	205.6	1725	-3.9	B11
Water Alert (↓): 13.0m						

SOUTHERN CALIFORNIA

Landmark	Facilities	Diff	S->N	Elev	Gra	Map
Water Alert (↑): 20.7m						
Falls Creek Road	R	1.1	206.7	1225	-4.9	B11
Snow Creek Road 3S01	R	0.1	206.8	1230	0.5	B11
Crossing jeep roads	R	0.7	207.5	1195	-0.5	B11
Cross good gravel road	R	0.4	207.9	1210	0.4	B11
Join good dirt road	R	0.7	208.6	1265	0.9	B11
Headwaters of Stubble Canyon Creek	—	0.8	209.4	1320	0.7	B11
Tamarack Road	R	0.2	209.6	1360	2.2	B11
General Delivery Cabazon, CA 92230 (951) 849-6233	PO,w,G,M,r,R: 4.50m W	0.0	209.6	1360	2.2	B11
Second powerline road	R	0.5	210.1	1475	2.5	C1
Buried Colorado River Aqueduct	—	0.4	210.5	1580	2.8	C1
Cottonwood Road	R	0.6	211.1	1690	2.0	C1
Cross 2 side-by-side roads	R	0.5	211.6	1850	3.5	C1
Gold Canyon Road	R	0.2	211.8	1845	-0.3	C1
Dirt road	R	2.0	213.8	2470	3.4	C1
Narrow pass between Gold and Teutang Canyons	—	1.2	215.0	3225	6.8	C1
Teutang Canyon	—	0.7	215.7	2815	-6.4	C1
Old jeep road in Whitewater Canyon, close to Whitewater Creek	w,R	2.9	218.6	2285	-2.0	C1
Water Alert (↑): 13.0m						
Two good camps	w	1.4	220.0	2605	2.5	C2
Ridgetop	—	1.2	221.2	3075	4.3	C2
West Fork Mission Creek Road	R	0.6	221.8	2918	-2.8	C2
Veers from dirt road	R	0.2	222.0	3010	5.0	C2
East Fork Mission Creek Road	R	3.5	225.5	3060	0.2	C2
Cross East Fork Mission Creek	w	0.5	226.0	3120	1.3	C2

SOUTHERN CALIFORNIA

Landmark	Facilities	Diff	S->N	Elev	Gra	Map
End of the dirt road next to East Fork of Mission Creek	w,R	0.9	226.9	3360	2.9	C3
Cross Mission Creek	w	4.9	231.8	4830	3.3	C3
Creekside camp	w	3.2	235.0	6110	4.3	C4
Jeep road built for logging	—	4.0	239.0	7850	4.7	C4
Meet Road 1N93 with MISSION CREEK TRAIL CAMP sign	R	0.3	239.3	7965	4.2	C4
Road 1N05	R	0.6	239.9	8240	5.0	C4
Road 1N05 crossing in a saddle	R	0.6	240.5	8115	-2.3	C4
Junction with CRHT-marked trail to Heart Bar Creek, early spring-time	w: 0.50m NW	1.5	242.0	7980	-1.0	C4
Water Alert (↓): 13.9m						
Road 1N96	R	2.5	244.5	8510	2.3	C4
Road junction east of Peak 8588	R	0.5	245.0	8340	-3.7	C4
Coon Creek Road 1N02	w,R: 1.50m W	1.2	246.2	8090	-2.3	C4
Reach a perpendicular trail	—	1.5	247.7	8610	3.8	C4
Cross dirt road	R	0.6	248.3	8635	0.5	C4
Cross jeep road	R	0.6	248.9	8390	-4.4	C4
Better dirt road	R	0.3	249.2	8260	-4.7	C4
Four roads and a trail	R	0.6	249.8	8100	-2.9	C4
Junction	—	1.0	250.8	8440	3.7	C4
Dirt road just east of Highway 38 & Onyx Summit	R	1.1	251.9	8510	0.7	C4
Road 1N01	R	1.0	252.9	8635	1.4	C5
Broom Flat Road 2N01	R	2.1	255.0	7885	-3.9	C5
Arrastre Trail Camp at Deer Spring	w	0.9	255.9	7605	-3.4	C5
Water Alert (↑): 14.4m						
Road 2N04	R	1.5	257.4	7155	-3.3	C5
Arrastre Creek Road 2N02	R	3.8	261.2	6775	-1.1	C6

SOUTHERN CALIFORNIA

Landmark	Facilities	Diff	S->N	Elev	Gra	Map
Highway 18	R	4.1	265.3	6829	0.1	C6
Doble Road 3N08	R	2.0	267.3	6855	0.1	C7
Unsigned spur trail down to Doble Trail Camp	w: 0.13m E	0.5	267.8	6880	0.5	C7
Second jeep road	w,R: 0.67m N	4.3	272.1	7630	1.9	C7
Cross a better road	R	0.3	272.4	7560	-2.5	C7
Van Dusen Canyon Road 3N09 next to Caribou Creek	w,R	1.7	274.1	7260	-1.9	C7
General Delivery Big Bear City, CA 92314 (909) 585-7132	PO,w,G,M,L,r, R: 3.00m SE	0.0	274.1	7260	-1.9	C7
Bertha Peak, first jeep road	R	1.6	275.7	7720	3.1	C8
Bertha Peak, second jeep road	R	0.7	276.4	7735	0.2	C8
Cougar Crest Trail 1E22	—	0.4	276.8	7680	-1.5	C8
Holcomb Valley Road 2N09	R	0.8	277.6	7550	-1.8	C8
Road 3N12, atop a saddle, junction to Delamar Spring	w,R: 0.90m W	2.6	280.2	7755	0.9	C8
Cross dirt road	R	0.8	281.0	7610	-2.0	C8
Cross jeep road	R	1.1	282.1	7305	-3.0	C8
Little Bear Springs Trail Camp	w	2.5	284.6	6600	-3.1	C9
Holcomb Creek	w	0.3	284.9	6510	-3.3	C9
Reach a saddle	—	2.0	286.9	6485	-0.1	C9
Cross a dirt road	R	0.8	287.7	6350	-1.8	C9
Crab Flats Road 3N16	R	3.5	291.2	5465	-2.7	C10
Cross Holcomb Creek	—	0.2	291.4	5430	-1.9	C10
Cienega Redonda Trail, next to Cienega Redonda Fork of Holcomb Creek	w	1.0	292.4	5325	-1.1	C10
Junction with Hawes Ranch Trail	w	0.4	292.8	5230	-2.6	C10
Holcomb Crossing Trail Camp	w	0.3	293.1	5190	-1.4	C10
90-foot steel-and-wood bridge spanning Deep Creek	w	4.1	297.2	4580	-1.6	C11

SOUTHERN CALIFORNIA

Landmark	Facilities	Diff	S->N	Elev	Gra	Map
General Delivery Cedar Glen, CA 92321 (909) 337-4614	PO,w,G,M,L, R: 4.30m SW	0.0	297.2	4580	-1.6	C11
Bacon Flats Road 3N20	R	2.6	299.8	4255	-1.4	C11
Deep Creek Hot Spring	w	6.8	306.6	3535	-1.1	C12
Cross Deep Creek via bridge	—	2.0	308.6	3315	-1.2	C12
Mojave River Forks Reservoir Dam	—	3.0	311.6	3131	-0.7	C13
Deep Creek ford	w	0.5	312.1	2990	-3.1	C13
Torn-up paved road	R	0.6	312.7	3010	0.4	C13
Highway 173	R	0.4	313.1	3190	4.9	C13
Little-used jeep road	R	0.4	313.5	3205	0.4	C13
Trailside spring	w	1.7	315.2	3470	1.7	C13
Jeep road atop a saddle	R	1.5	316.7	3430	-0.3	C14
Grass Valley Creek	w	0.3	317.0	3330	-3.6	C14
Steep jeep road	R	0.7	317.7	3480	2.3	C14
North-descending jeep road halfway to Silverwood Lake	w,G,R: 0.30m NW	2.6	320.3	3480	0.0	C14
Road 2N33	R	2.2	322.5	3400	-0.4	C14
Poorly paved road	R	0.4	322.9	3170	-6.3	C14
Highway 173	R	0.3	323.2	3175	0.2	C14
Very poor dirt road south of Mojave Siphon Power Plant	R	0.5	323.7	3200	0.5	C15
First saddle in Silverwood Lake State Recreation	—	0.6	324.3	3460	4.7	C15
Unsigned spur trail to Garces Overlook	—	2.5	326.8	3580	0.5	C15
Cross jeep road	R	0.8	327.6	3455	-1.7	C15
Two-lane bike path to Cleghorn Picnic Area	w: 0.50m E	0.7	328.3	3390	-1.0	C15
Signed junction to group-camp complex	—	0.1	328.4	3380	-1.1	C15

SOUTHERN CALIFORNIA

Landmark	Facilities	Diff	S->N	Elev	Gra	Map
Silverwood Lake State Recreation Area's entrance road	w,G,M,sh,R: 1.70m E	0.1	328.5	3390	1.1	C15
Offramp, west	—	0.1	328.6	3395	0.5	C15
Small picnic area	—	0.4	329.0	3440	1.2	C15
Narrow paved road to water tank	R	0.4	329.4	3530	2.4	C15
Leave SRA and join jeep road	R	2.2	331.6	4040	2.5	C15
Road atop viewful Cleghorn Ridge	R	0.3	331.9	4160	4.3	C15
Small stream	w	0.9	332.8	3830	-4.0	C15
Little Horsethief Canyon's dry creek bed	—	2.8	335.6	3570	-1.0	C16
Road under a huge power-transmission line	R	2.5	338.1	3840	1.2	C17
Cross Road 3N44	R	2.4	340.5	3355	-2.2	C17
Cross another road	R	0.4	340.9	3300	-1.5	C17
Descending dirt road	R	0.2	341.1	3265	-1.9	C17
Better dirt road, end of descent	R	0.3	341.4	3140	-4.5	C17
Crowder Canyon	w	0.3	341.7	3045	-3.4	C17
Water Alert (↓): 23.1m						
Road before Interstate 15 in Cajon Canyon	R	0.4	342.1	3000	-1.2	C17
Best Western Inn Attn: (Your Name) PCT Hiker 8317 US Highway 138 Phelan, CA 92371 (760) 249-6777	w,G,M,L, R: 0.60m NW	0.0	342.1	3000	-1.2	C17
PCT trail resumes	—	0.4	342.5	2930	-1.9	D1
Southern Pacific Railroad tracks	—	0.8	343.3	3020	1.2	D1
Road 3N78, second powerline road	R	1.2	344.5	3360	3.1	D1
Swarthout Canyon Road 3N28	R	2.9	347.4	3560	0.7	D1
Jeep road	R	0.5	347.9	3700	3.0	D1
Sharpless Ranch Road 3N29	R	4.1	352.0	5150	3.8	D2

SOUTHERN CALIFORNIA

Landmark	Facilities	Diff	S->N	Elev	Gra	Map
Gap in the ridge	—	0.9	352.9	5260	1.3	D2
Sheep Creek Truck Road 3N31	R	3.5	356.4	6300	3.2	D2
Viewpoint on ridge-top flat	—	0.2	356.6	6350	2.7	D2
Roadend just east of Gobber's Knob	R	0.8	357.4	6480	1.8	D2
Jeep road atop Blue Ridge	R	4.4	361.8	8115	4.0	D3
Posted trailhead	—	0.1	361.9	8176	6.6	D3
Acorn Canyon Trail	—	1.7	363.6	8250	0.5	D3
General Delivery Wrightwood, CA 92397 (760) 249-8882	PO,w,G,M,L, R: 4.50m N	0.0	363.6	8250	0.5	D3
Guffy Campground	w: 0.15m N	1.0	364.6	8225	-0.3	D3
Water Alert (↑): 22.9m						
Dirt road beside an artificial lake	R	2.2	366.8	8115	-0.5	D4
PCT pathway on the west side of the reservoir	—	0.1	366.9	8120	0.5	D4
Road 3N06	R	0.4	367.3	7955	-4.5	D4
Blue Ridge Campground	—	0.1	367.4	7910	-4.9	D4
Angeles Crest Highway 2	R	2.1	369.5	7386	-2.7	D4
Grassy Hollow Family Campground	w	1.0	370.5	7300	-0.9	D4
Spur to walk-in Jackson Flat Group Campground	—	1.1	371.6	7480	1.8	D5
Road 3N26	R	1.6	373.2	7220	-1.8	D5
Vincent Gap	—	0.8	374.0	6585	-8.6	D5
Side trail to Lamel Spring	w: 0.06m S	1.7	375.7	7765	7.6	D5
Mt. Baden-Powell Spur Trail	—	2.3	378.0	9245	7.0	D5
Lateral trail to Lily Spring	w: 0.33m N	3.9	381.9	8540	-2.0	D6
Windy Gap	—	1.8	383.7	7588	-5.7	D6
Little Jimmy Spring	w	0.1	383.8	7460	-14.0	D6
Little Jimmy Campground	—	0.2	384.0	7450	-0.5	D6

SOUTHERN CALIFORNIA

Landmark	Facilities	Diff	S->N	Elev	Gra	Map
Cross Road/Trail 3N04	R	1.1	385.1	7360	-0.9	D6
Angeles Crest Highway 2	R	1.0	386.1	6670	-7.5	D6
Mt. Williamson Summit Trail	—	1.7	387.8	7900	7.9	D6
Angeles Crest Highway 2	R	1.5	389.3	6700	-8.7	D6
Eagles Roost Picnic Area	—	0.9	390.2	6650	-0.6	D7
Rattlesnake Trail 10W03	—	1.3	391.5	6165	-4.1	D7
Little Rock Creek	w	0.3	391.8	6080	-3.1	D7
Burkhart Trail 10W02 next to Little Rock Creek	w	2.0	393.8	5640	-2.4	D7
Leave Burkhart Trail	—	0.3	394.1	5730	3.3	D7
Cooper Canyon Trail Campground	w	1.2	395.3	6240	4.6	D7
Climb to a gap east of Winston Peak	—	1.0	396.3	6700	5.0	D7
Dirt road to Cooper Canyon Trail Campground	R	0.6	396.9	6640	-1.1	D7
Headwaters of Cooper Canyon Creek	w	0.4	397.3	6530	-3.0	D7
Cloudburst Summit	—	0.8	398.1	7018	6.6	D7
Second highway crossing below a hairpin turn	R	0.8	398.9	6735	-3.8	D8
Road junction in Cloudburst Canyon	R	0.6	399.5	6545	-3.4	D8
Camp Glenwood	w	1.2	400.7	6400	-1.3	D8
Highway 2	R	0.5	401.2	6320	-1.7	D8
Three Points on Angeles Crest Highway	R	2.0	403.2	5885	-2.4	D8
Unused dirt road	R	1.5	404.7	5760	-0.9	D8
Another dirt road leads to Pasadena Camp	R	0.2	404.9	5655	-5.7	D8
Signed trail junction, hikers left, horses right	—	1.9	406.8	5240	-2.4	D8
Sulphur Springs Campground	w: 0.20m E	0.1	406.9	5200	-4.3	D8

SOUTHERN CALIFORNIA

Landmark	Facilities	Diff	S->N	Elev	Gra	Map
Merge with the foot trail	—	0.5	407.4	5265	1.4	D8
Little Rock Creek Road 5N04	R	0.2	407.6	5320	3.0	D8
Gap at the head of Bare Mountain Canyon	—	2.4	410.0	5830	2.3	D8
Shaded Fiddleneck Spring	w	0.6	410.6	6240	7.4	D9
Fountainhead Spring	w	0.5	411.1	6440	4.3	D9
Ridgetop vista point	—	1.3	412.4	6760	2.7	D9
Shady gap near Pacifico Mountain Campground	—	0.7	413.1	6645	-1.8	D9
Jeep road	R	1.6	414.7	6380	-1.8	D9
Trail resumes	—	0.4	415.1	6210	-4.6	D9
Signed spur trail to Pacifico Mountain Road 3N17 trailhead	w,R	3.4	418.5	4980	-3.9	D9
Mill Creek Summit, Ranger Station	w	0.2	418.7	4910	-3.8	D9
Cross Mt. Gleason Road	R	2.5	421.2	5590	3.0	D10
Signed side trail	—	3.1	424.3	5640	0.2	D10
Road 4N24	R	0.6	424.9	5500	-2.5	D10
Shady campsite just below the trail	—	0.8	425.7	5195	-4.1	D10
Junction with a south-branching trail	—	3.8	429.5	6360	3.3	D11
Mt. Gleason's north ridge	—	0.4	429.9	6410	1.4	D11
Messenger Flats Campground	w	0.8	430.7	5870	-7.3	D11
Moody Canyon Road	R	1.5	432.2	5320	-4.0	D11
Santa Clara Divide Road	R	1.2	433.4	5425	0.9	D11
PCT trail resumes	—	0.1	433.5	5395	-3.3	D11
West-descending jeep track	—	0.7	434.2	5395	0.0	D12
BPL Road 4N32 Nork Fork Saddle Ranger Station	w,R	2.0	436.2	4210	-6.4	D12
Mattox Canyon creek	w	4.0	440.2	2685	-4.1	D12
Cross Indian Canyon Road 4N37	R	2.9	443.1	2640	-0.2	D13

SOUTHERN CALIFORNIA

Landmark	Facilities	Diff	S->N	Elev	Gra	Map
Soledad Canyon Road	R	1.1	444.2	2237	-4.0	D13
General Delivery Acton, CA 93510 (661) 269-8618	PO,w,G,M, R: 5.80m E	0.0	444.2	2237	-4.0	D13
Santa Clara River ford	w	0.1	444.3	2205	-3.5	D13
Southern Pacific Railroad tracks	—	0.2	444.5	2243	2.1	D13
Saddle out of the canyon	—	0.4	444.9	2485	6.6	D13
Young Canyon Road	R	1.3	446.2	2960	4.0	D13
Gap near the head of Bobcat Canyon	—	0.7	446.9	2780	-2.8	D13
Jeep road separating Soledad and Escondido Canyons	R	1.6	448.5	3160	2.6	D13
Saddle during the descent	—	0.5	449.0	2960	-4.3	D13
Canyon bottom	—	1.9	450.9	2400	-3.2	D13
Antelope Valley Freeway 14	R	0.1	451.0	2370	-3.3	D13
Cross to the canyon's north side	—	0.8	451.8	2335	-0.5	D13
Junction with VRCP trail	—	0.1	451.9	2323	-1.3	D13
Junction on dirt road, descending west	R	0.7	452.6	2435	1.7	D13
Gate at a large parking area	—	0.2	452.8	2485	2.7	D13
Escondido Canyon Road	R	0.7	453.5	2510	0.4	D13
Aqua Dulce Canyon Road	R	0.4	453.9	2470	-1.1	D13
Darling Road (downtown Aqua Dulce)	w,G,M,R	0.5	454.4	2530	1.3	D13
Water Alert (↓): 24.4m						
Old Sierra Highway	R	1.8	456.2	2725	1.2	E2
Mint Canyon Road	R	0.1	456.3	2730	0.5	E2
Petersen Road	R	0.2	456.5	2755	1.4	E2
Dirt road	R	0.1	456.6	2750	-0.5	E2
Angeles National Forest boundary	—	0.4	457.0	2905	4.2	E3
Mint Canyon step-across creek	—	1.5	458.5	2865	-0.3	E3

SOUTHERN CALIFORNIA

Landmark	Facilities	Diff	S->N	Elev	Gra	Map
Big Tree Trail 14W02	—	1.1	459.6	3330	4.6	E3
Sierra Pelona Ridge Road 6N07	R	2.7	462.3	4500	4.7	E3
Up to a low saddle	—	0.3	462.6	4555	2.0	E3
Bear Spring	—	0.7	463.3	4350	-3.2	E3
Ridgetop-firebreak jeep trail	—	0.7	464.0	3995	-5.5	E3
Junction with the old PCT trail	—	0.6	464.6	3785	-3.8	E3
Bouquet Canyon Road 6N05	R	1.0	465.6	3340	-4.8	E3
Old California Riding and Hiking Trail (CRHT)	—	2.7	468.3	3985	2.6	E3
Pass with another firebreak above Leona Divide Road	R	1.3	469.6	4300	2.6	E5
Road 6N09	R	2.0	471.6	3725	-3.1	E5
Ridge with a firebreak	—	2.2	473.8	3815	0.4	E5
San Francisquito Canyon Road	w,R: 0.15m SW	4.8	478.6	3385	-1.0	E5
Water Alert (↑): 24.2m						
Dirt road above San Francisquito Canyon	R	0.4	479.0	3520	3.7	E5
Grass Mountain Road	R	1.2	480.2	4275	6.8	E5
Saddle where 4 dirt roads converge	R	1.4	481.6	3900	-2.9	E6
Tule Canyon Road 7N01	R	1.3	482.9	3900	0.0	E6
Lake Hughes Road 7N09	R	3.4	486.3	3050	-2.7	E6
General Delivery Lake Hughes, CA 93532 (661) 724-9281	PO,w,G,M,L,sh, r,R: 2.20m NE	0.0	486.3	3050	-2.7	E6
Trailside wet-season spring	w	1.4	487.7	3710	5.1	E6
Water Alert (↓): 30.7m						
Sawmill-Liebre Firebreak	—	0.7	488.4	4190	7.5	E6
Maxwell Truck Trail 7N08	—	2.0	490.4	4505	1.7	E7
Cross 2 dirt roads	R	3.1	493.5	4680	0.6	E7

SOUTHERN CALIFORNIA

Landmark	Facilities	Diff	S->N	Elev	Gra	Map
Ascend to a trail intersection with Upper Shake Campground	w: 0.60m N	0.5	494.0	4805	2.7	E7
Ridgetop road junction above Shake Canyon	R	2.8	496.8	5245	1.7	E7
Ridgenose to a junction with a spur trail to Sawmill Campground	—	2.0	498.8	5015	-1.2	E8
Road crossing	R	1.2	500.0	4790	-2.0	E8
Atmore Meadows Spur Road 7N19	w,R: 1.70m SW	0.7	500.7	4705	-1.3	E8
Up to a grassy saddle	—	2.0	502.7	5655	5.2	E8
Spur trail to waterless Bear Campground	—	2.1	504.8	5370	-1.5	E9
Liebre Mountain Truck Trail 7N23	—	0.3	505.1	5545	6.3	E9
North-descending dirt road	R	0.9	506.0	5580	0.4	E9
Jeep road	R	1.2	507.2	5745	1.5	E9
Dirt road	R	0.1	507.3	5720	-2.7	E9
Jeep track ends	—	1.0	508.3	5140	-6.3	E9
Levels out at a dirt road spur	R	2.5	510.8	3995	-5.0	E9
Small pond	—	0.6	511.4	3810	-3.3	E9
Pine Canyon Road	R	0.3	511.7	3845	1.3	E9
Cross a jeep road	R	3.8	515.5	3522	-0.9	E10
Over-engineered switchbacks to merge with a good jeep road	R	2.1	517.6	3175	-1.8	E10
Highway 138	w,R	0.8	518.4	3040	-1.8	E10
Water Alert (↓): 16.4m						
Water Alert (↑): 30.7m						
Hikertown c/o Richard Skaggs Attn: (Your Name) PCT Hiker 26803 W. Avenue C-15 Lancaster, CA 93536 (661) 724-0086	w,G,sh,r, R: 0.10m NE	0.0	518.4	3040	-1.8	E10

SOUTHERN CALIFORNIA

Landmark	Facilities	Diff	S->N	Elev	Gra	Map
Gil's Country Store Star Route 138, 28105 Highway 138 Lancaster, CA 93536-9207 (805) 724-9097	w,G,r: 1.30m W	0.0	518.4	3040	-1.8	E10
Neenach School Road	R	0.5	518.9	2992	-1.0	E10
Pavement ends	—	0.3	519.2	2970	-0.8	E10
Pair of roads that bridge the aqueduct at a siphon	R	1.0	520.2	2965	-0.1	E10
Los Angeles Aqueduct, turning east	—	0.3	520.5	2965	0.0	E10
Straight-north course turns east	—	3.2	523.7	3090	0.4	E11
Intersection with a good dirt road after Little Oak Canyon Creek	R	5.5	529.2	3110	0.0	E12
Ignore dirt road, continue on better road	R	3.0	532.2	2893	-0.8	E12
Triangular junction	—	0.4	532.6	2915	0.6	E12
Los Angeles Aqueduct, underground	—	0.6	533.2	3105	3.4	E12
Cottonwood Creek bridge, check opening on aqueduct for water access	w	1.6	534.8	3120	0.1	E12
Water Alert (↓): 23.2m						
Water Alert (↑): 16.5m						
Next dirt road	R	0.1	534.9	3120	0.0	E12
Resumption of PCT trail	—	0.4	535.3	3160	1.1	E12
Bike path overlooking Cottonwood Creek	—	0.5	535.8	3250	2.0	E12
East-west jeep road	R	1.0	536.8	3465	2.3	E12
T junction, poor dirt roads	R	0.5	537.3	3609	3.1	E12
Up to a viewful and breezy knoll	—	0.4	537.7	3800	5.2	E13
Poor jeep road that traces the south boundary of a barbed-wire fence	R	0.2	537.9	3790	-0.5	E13

SOUTHERN CALIFORNIA

Landmark	Facilities	Diff	S->N	Elev	Gra	Map
Join good jeep road	R	0.7	538.6	4070	4.3	E13
End of the fence	—	0.3	538.9	4120	1.8	E13
Rough jeep/dirtbike path, west of Tylerhorse Canyon	—	2.2	541.1	4960	4.1	E13
Tylerhorse Canyon	—	0.3	541.4	4840	-4.3	E13
Saddle overlooking Gamble Spring Canyon	—	2.9	544.3	4960	0.4	E13
Gamble Spring Canyon	—	0.6	544.9	4625	-6.1	E13
Cross a jeep road	R	3.1	548.0	6070	5.1	E13
Headwaters of Burnham and Pitney canyons	—	2.8	550.8	5980	-0.3	E14
Cross Oak Creek via steel bridge	w	7.2	558.0	4075	-2.9	E15
Water Alert (↓): 25.4m						
Water Alert (↑): 23.2m						
Paved Tehachapi-Willow Springs Road	R	0.3	558.3	4150	2.7	E15
General Delivery Tehachapi, CA 93581 (661) 822-0279	PO,w,G,M,L,r, R: 9.40m W	0.0	558.3	4150	2.7	E15
General Delivery Mojave, CA 93502 (661) 824-3502	PO,w,G,M,L,r, R: 12.00m E	0.0	558.3	4150	2.7	E15
One good dirt road with plastic marker-posts	R	0.7	559.0	4165	0.2	E15
Second dirt road	R	0.2	559.2	4160	-0.3	E15
Up to a small saddle	—	0.5	559.7	4495	7.3	E15
Viewful ridgetop	—	0.5	560.2	4560	1.4	E15
Fourth, good dirt road	R	1.6	561.8	4485	-0.5	E16
Down to a saddle with a poor dirt road	R	0.5	562.3	4600	2.5	E16
Cross a dirt road	R	0.9	563.2	4765	2.0	E16
Cameron Road	R	2.1	565.3	3905	-4.4	E16

SOUTHERN CALIFORNIA

Landmark	Facilities	Diff	S->N	Elev	Gra	Map
Atchison Topeka and Santa Fe and Southern Pacific Railroad tracks	—	0.5	565.8	3824	-1.8	E16
Tehachapi Pass (Highway 58), start of Sierra Nevada	R	0.8	566.6	3830	0.1	E16
Gate opposite the Cameron Road Exit 1 mile sign	R	1.2	567.8	3780	-0.5	F1
Trail end after the head of Waterfall Canyon	—	7.4	575.2	6120	3.4	F2
0.2 mile from the gated road, after the Sky River Ranch sign	R	3.9	579.1	6000	-0.3	F3
Golden Oaks Spring	w	4.3	583.4	5480	-1.3	F4
Water Alert (↓): 18.9m						
Water Alert (↑): 25.4m						
Cross a green gate in a cattle fence	—	6.7	590.1	5102	-0.6	F5
Cross below a camping area by an east-west road	R	3.1	593.2	5010	-0.3	F5
Hamp Williams Pass	—	3.5	596.7	5530	1.6	F5
Curve of a private dirt road	R	3.2	599.9	5620	0.3	F6
T junction	—	0.8	600.7	5996	5.1	F6
Ascend along a tight right curve, PCT path on left	—	0.4	601.1	6160	4.5	F6
Cross a dirt road leading to Robin Bird Spring	w,R: 0.10m W	1.1	602.2	6360	2.0	F7
Water Alert (↑): 18.8m						
Jawbone Canyon Road	R	0.4	602.6	6620	7.1	F7
Log footbridge over branch of Cottonwood Creek	w	1.8	604.4	6480	-0.8	F7
Logging road	R	1.0	605.4	6720	2.6	F7
Landers Creek	w: 0.20m W	1.9	607.3	6300	-2.4	F7
Piute Mountain Road	R	0.9	608.2	6220	-1.0	F7
SNF Road 29S05	w,R: 0.30m N	0.7	608.9	6300	1.2	F7

SOUTHERN CALIFORNIA

Landmark	Facilities	Diff	S->N	Elev	Gra	Map
Water Alert (↓): 35.5m						
Piute Mountain Road again, summit of Harris Grade	R	2.3	611.2	6620	1.5	F7
Kelso Valley Road at a pass	R	4.8	616.0	4953	-3.8	F9
Butterbredt Canyon Road, SC123 to a spring	w,R: 1.20m N	2.1	618.1	4540	-2.1	F9
Slopes of Pinyon Mountain, multi-road-and-path junction to Willow Spring, Road SC103	w,R: 1.80m NW	4.1	622.2	5283	2.0	F10
Another multi-road-and-trail junction	R	1.6	623.8	5382	0.7	F10
A ridgecrest saddle	—	1.1	624.9	5700	3.1	F10
Road SC328 on a crestline saddle	R	0.8	625.7	5300	-5.4	F10
Road SC47 on another crestline saddle	R	0.2	625.9	5380	4.3	F10
Road SC42	R	3.0	628.9	5740	1.3	F10
Junction at Bird Spring Pass	—	2.5	631.4	5355	-1.7	F11
Ridge with a westward orientation	—	2.4	633.8	6460	5.0	F11
Highest point before Walker Pass and beyond	—	1.3	635.1	6940	4.0	F11
Road to Yellow Jacket Spring	w,R: 0.70m NW	2.3	637.4	6260	-3.2	F11
Join the road to McIvers Spring	R	4.5	641.9	6670	1.0	F12
Junction to McIvers Spring	w: 0.30m E	2.2	644.1	6680	0.0	F12
Water Alert (↑): 35.5m						
Curve around a sharp canyon crease	—	3.0	647.1	6680	0.0	F13
Ridgeline saddle after Jacks Creek	—	2.2	649.3	5860	-4.0	F13
Path leading to Walker Pass Trailhead Campground	w: 0.10m N	2.1	651.4	5100	-3.9	F13
Water Alert (↓): 13.0m						
Historical Marker	—	0.6	652.0	5246	2.6	F13

SOUTHERN CALIFORNIA

Landmark	Facilities	Diff	S->N	Elev	Gra	Map
General Delivery Onyx, CA 93255 (760) 378-2121	PO,w,G,r, R: 17.60m W	0.0	652.0	5246	2.6	F13
Trailside medium-size campsite	—	2.2	654.2	6190	4.7	G1
North-facing slopes to a saddle	—	1.9	656.1	6585	2.3	G2
Morris/Jenkins saddle	—	0.8	656.9	6500	-1.2	G2
Commemorative plaque	—	0.3	657.2	6580	2.9	G2
Rounded point of a ridge	—	1.4	658.6	6950	2.9	G2
Jenkins/Owens saddle	—	2.2	660.8	7020	0.3	G1
A lesser saddle	—	1.4	662.2	6300	-5.6	G1
Rough dirt road	R	1.0	663.2	5500	-8.7	G1
Joshua Tree Spring	w: 0.25m SW	0.9	664.1	5360	-1.7	G1
Water Alert (↑): 12.8m						
Cross a ridge at a saddle	—	1.2	665.3	5240	-1.1	G1
Northwest to another saddle	—	1.4	666.7	5860	4.8	G3
Branch of Spanish Needle Creek	w	1.9	668.6	5160	-4.0	G3
Spring-fed branch of Spanish Needle Creek	w	0.4	669.0	5300	3.8	G3
Spring-fed streamlet	w	0.7	669.7	5560	4.0	G3
Spanish Needle Creek (3rd encounter)	w	0.6	670.3	5620	1.1	G3
Ridge between Spanish Needle Group and Lamont Peak	—	2.9	673.2	6800	4.4	G4
Second broader saddle	—	3.4	676.6	6900	0.3	G4
Sierra crest saddle with limited views	—	1.4	678.0	6260	-5.0	G4
Seasonal creek	—	0.8	678.8	5950	-4.2	G4
Canebrake Road	w,R: 0.30m NE	2.5	681.3	5555	-1.7	G4
Fox Mill Spring	w	2.3	683.6	6580	4.8	G4
Dirt road	R	0.1	683.7	6580	0.0	G4
Trail summit	—	4.0	687.7	8020	3.9	G5

SOUTHERN CALIFORNIA

Landmark	Facilities	Diff	S->N	Elev	Gra	Map
Road crossing	R	0.2	687.9	7980	-2.2	G5
Long Valley Loop Road	R	1.7	689.6	7220	-4.9	G5
Spur ridge; last camp before Rockhouse Basin	—	2.6	692.2	6600	-2.6	G6
First creek after Rockhouse Basin (Manter Creek)	w	1.8	694.0	5845	-4.6	G6
Seasonal creek	w	3.4	697.4	5870	0.1	G6
South Fork Kern River	w	1.4	698.8	5760	-0.9	G7
Stream	w	1.6	700.4	5916	1.1	G7
Closed OHV road	R	0.6	701.0	5980	1.2	G7
Bridge near Kennedy Meadows general store	—	1.8	702.8	6020	0.2	G7
Kennedy Meadows General Store P.O. Box 3A-5 Inyokern, CA 93527	w,G,r,R: 0.70m SE	0.0	702.8	6020	0.2	G7

CENTRAL CALIFORNIA

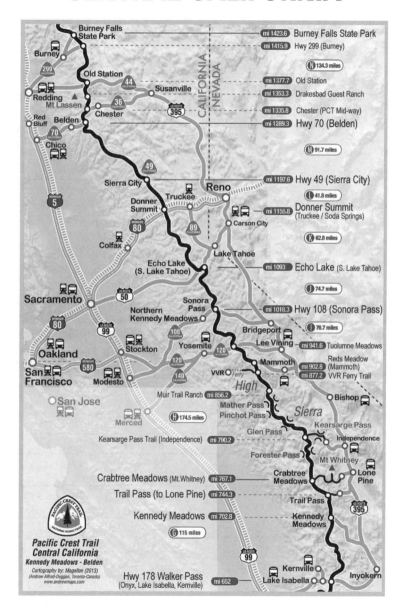

Burney Falls State Park
Burney
Old Station
Susanville
Redding
Mt Lassen
Chester
Red Bluff
Belden
Chico
Sierra City
Donner Summit
Truckee
Reno
Carson City
Colfax
Echo Lake (S. Lake Tahoe)
Lake Tahoe
Sacramento
Northern Kennedy Meadows
Sonora Pass
Bridgeport
Oakland
Stockton
Yosemite
Lee Vining
San Francisco
Modesto
Mammoth
VVR Ferry
Reds Meadow (Mammoth)
VVR Ferry Trail
Muir Trail Ranch
San Jose
Merced
Mather Pass
Pinchot Pass
High Sierra
Bishop
Kearsarge Pass
Kearsarge Pass Trail (Independence)
Glen Pass
Independence
Forester Pass
Mt Whitney
Crabtree Meadows (Mt.Whitney)
Crabtree Meadows
Lone Pine
Trail Pass (to Lone Pine)
Trail Pass
Kennedy Meadows
Kennedy Meadows
Kernville
Inyokern
Hwy 178 Walker Pass (Onyx, Lake Isabella, Kernville)
Lake Isabella

mi 1423.6 Burney Falls State Park
mi 1415.9 Hwy 299 (Burney)
134.3 miles
mi 1377.7 Old Station
mi 1353.3 Drakesbad Guest Ranch
mi 1335.8 Chester (PCT Mid-way)
mi 1289.3 Hwy 70 (Belden)
91.7 miles
mi 1197.6 Hwy 49 (Sierra City)
41.8 miles
mi 1155.8 Donner Summit (Truckee / Soda Springs)
62.8 miles
mi 1093 Echo Lake (S. Lake Tahoe)
74.7 miles
mi 1018.3 Hwy 108 (Sonora Pass)
76.7 miles
mi 941.6 Tuolumne Meadows
mi 902.8 Reds Meadow (Mammoth)
mi 877.2 VVR Ferry Trail
mi 856.2
174.5 miles
Kearsarge Pass Trail (Independence) mi 790.2
mi 767.1
mi 744.3
mi 702.8
115 miles
mi 652

CALIFORNIA
NEVADA

Pacific Crest Trail
Central California
Kennedy Meadows - Belden
Cartography by: Magellan (2013)
(Andrew Alfred-Duggan, Toronto-Canada)
www.andrewmaps.com

CENTRAL CALIFORNIA

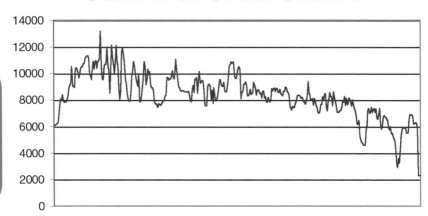

**Elevation Profile for Central California
From Kennedy Meadows to Belden**

Section Total Mileage: 586.5 miles

Landmark	Facilities	Diff	S->N	Elev	Gra	Map
Cross road to campground	R	1.8	704.6	6080	0.4	G7
Cross road again	R	0.4	705.0	6120	1.1	G7
Kennedy Meadows Campground	w	0.2	705.2	6150	1.6	G7
Junction leaving Clover Meadow Trail	—	1.1	706.3	6240	0.9	G8
Steel-girdered wooden bridge	w	0.8	707.1	6300	0.8	G8
Crag Creek	w	2.0	709.1	6810	2.8	G8
Junction with the old Clover Meadow Trail	—	2.5	711.6	7560	3.3	G8
T junction with Haiwee Trail 37E01	—	1.1	712.7	8060	4.9	G8
Beck Meadows Trail 35E01	—	0.4	713.1	7953	-2.9	G8
Deer Mountain's northern ridge	—	2.2	715.3	8390	2.2	G9
Low, broad ridge	—	1.0	716.3	7940	-4.9	G9

CENTRAL CALIFORNIA

Landmark	Facilities	Diff	S->N	Elev	Gra	Map
South Fork Kern River bridge in Monache Meadows	w	0.4	716.7	7820	-3.3	G9
Southeast-heading trail to Kennedy Meadows	—	0.1	716.8	7840	2.2	G9
Right turn at a junction	—	0.1	716.9	7840	0.0	G9
Low ridge	—	1.2	718.1	8050	1.9	G9
Cow Creek	w	1.3	719.4	8260	1.8	G10
Olancha Pass Trail	—	1.2	720.6	8920	6.0	G10
Trail junction after Cow Creek	w	0.5	721.1	9090	3.7	G10
North to a lateral	—	0.2	721.3	9240	8.2	G10
After Monache Creek bowl, levels off on a saddle	—	3.4	724.7	10540	4.2	G10
Cross a year-round creek	w	3.7	728.4	9030	-4.4	G11
Meadowside trail at a causeway abutment	—	0.7	729.1	9010	-0.3	G11
Ford a step-across all-year Death Canyon creek	w	1.7	730.8	8940	-0.4	G11
Crestline saddle	—	3.7	734.5	10390	4.3	G11
Junction with a faint half-mile-long lateral to a spring	w: 0.30m N	1.5	736.0	10425	0.3	G11
Second saddle with path signed CORRAL	w: 0.20m E	1.6	737.6	10260	-1.1	G12
Descend northwest to an obscure path	—	1.8	739.4	10000	-1.6	G12
Sierra crest at a low saddle to Diaz Creek	w: 0.50m E	1.8	741.2	9670	-2.0	G12
CORRAL junction sign	w: 0.20m N	1.3	742.5	9960	2.4	G12
Mulkey Pass	—	1.5	744.0	10380	3.0	G12
Junction with Trail Pass Trail	—	0.8	744.8	10500	1.6	G12
General Delivery Lone Pine, CA 93545 (760) 876-5681	PO,w,G,M,L,r, R: 24.90m E	0.0	744.8	10500	1.6	G12
Path to Poison Meadow	—	1.3	746.1	10740	2.0	G13

CENTRAL CALIFORNIA

Landmark	Facilities	Diff	S->N	Elev	Gra	Map
Intersect the crest at a saddle	—	0.6	746.7	10740	0.0	G13
Cottonwood Pass	—	2.9	749.6	11160	1.6	G13
Chicken Spring Lake outlet	w	0.6	750.2	11235	1.4	G13
Seasonal creek	w	2.5	752.7	11320	0.4	G14
Sequoia National Park border	—	0.6	753.3	11320	0.0	G14
Siberian Pass/Rock Creek trail	—	0.9	754.2	11139	-2.2	G14
Down to a junction with Rock Creek Trail	—	4.9	759.1	9959	-2.6	G14
Cross a brook	w	0.3	759.4	9840	-4.3	G14
Rock Creek crossing	w	0.9	760.3	9550	-3.5	G15
Guyot Creek	w	1.5	761.8	10320	5.6	G15
Pass northeast of 12,300-foot Mt. Guyot	—	1.0	762.8	10920	6.5	G15
Crabtree Meadow with lateral to Mt. Whitney	w	3.5	766.3	10329	-1.8	G15
Path north-northwest to a signed junction with JMT to Mt. Whitney		0.8	767.1	10870	7.4	G15
Sandy Meadow to a high saddle	—	1.7	768.8	10964	0.6	H2
Wallace Creek and High Sierra Trail junction	w	1.6	770.4	10390	-3.9	H2
Ford of Wright Creek	w	1.1	771.5	10790	3.9	H2
Shepherd Pass Trail	w	3.5	775.0	10930	0.4	H2
Lake South America Trail	—	0.7	775.7	11160	3.6	H2
Forester Pass	—	4.3	780.0	13180	5.1	H3
Center Basin trail	w	4.5	784.5	10500	-6.5	H3
Vidette Meadow	w	2.8	787.3	9600	-3.5	H4
Junction up Bubbs Creek canyon	—	0.7	788.0	9550	-0.8	H4
Bullfrog Lake junction	—	1.5	789.5	10530	7.1	H4
Kearsarge Pass trails	—	0.7	790.2	10710	2.8	H4

CENTRAL CALIFORNIA

Landmark	Facilities	Diff	S->N	Elev	Gra	Map
General Delivery Independence, CA 93526 (760) 878-2210	PO,w,G,M,L,r, R: 24.00m E	0.0	790.2	10710	2.8	H4
Glen Pass	—	2.3	792.5	11978	6.0	H4
Sixty Lakes Trail Junction	w	2.0	794.5	10550	-7.8	H4
Dragon Lake Trail Junction	—	0.4	794.9	10560	0.3	H4
Rae Lakes Ranger Station Junction	—	0.2	795.1	10600	2.2	H4
Arrowhead Lake	w	1.6	796.7	10300	-2.0	H4
Dollar Lake (unsigned Baxter Pass Trail)	w	0.4	797.1	10230	-1.9	H4
Woods Creek	w	3.7	800.8	8492	-5.1	H5
Sawmill Pass Trail	w	3.4	804.2	10370	6.0	H5
Pinchot Pass	—	3.7	807.9	12130	5.2	H5
Lake Marjorie	w	1.7	809.6	11160	-6.2	H6
Taboose Pass Trail	w	1.3	810.9	10750	-3.4	H6
South Fork Kings River Trail	w	1.3	812.2	10050	-5.9	H6
South Fork Kings River ford	w	2.2	814.4	10840	3.9	H6
Mather Pass	—	3.0	817.4	12100	4.6	H7
Upper Palisade Lake	w	2.5	819.9	11000	-4.8	H7
Lower Palisade Lake	w	1.0	820.9	10600	-4.3	H7
Deer Meadow	w	3.0	823.9	8860	-6.3	H8
Middle Fork Kings River	w	3.7	827.6	8020	-2.5	H9
Bishop Pass Trail	w	3.3	830.9	8710	2.3	H9
Helen Lake	w	5.7	836.6	11595	5.5	H10
Muir Pass	—	1.3	837.9	11955	3.0	H10
Evolution Creek	w	2.2	840.1	11400	-2.7	H10
Evolution Lake Inlet	w	2.4	842.5	10850	-2.5	H10
McClure Meadow	w	4.9	847.4	9650	-2.7	H11
Evolution Creek crossing	w	2.5	849.9	9210	-1.9	H12

CENTRAL CALIFORNIA

Landmark	Facilities	Diff	S->N	Elev	Gra	Map
South Fork San Joaquin River	w	1.0	850.9	8470	-8.1	H12
Piute Pass Trail	w	3.5	854.4	8050	-1.3	H12
Florence Lake Trail	—	1.8	856.2	7890	-1.0	H13
Muir Trail Ranch Attn: (Your Name) PCT Hiker Box 176 Lakeshore, CA 93634-0176	w 1.50m NW;R	0.0	856.2	7890	-1.0	H13
Florence Lake Trail #2	—	1.7	857.9	8400	3.3	H13
Senger Creek	w	2.2	860.1	9740	6.6	H13
Unmaintained trail to South Fork of San Joaquin River	—	1.7	861.8	10140	2.6	H13
Sally Keyes Lakes	w	0.6	862.4	10200	1.1	H13
Heart Lake	w	0.8	863.2	10550	4.8	H14
Selden Pass	—	0.7	863.9	10900	5.4	H14
Marie Lake outlet	w	0.9	864.8	10570	-4.0	H14
Rosemarie Meadow	w	1.6	866.4	10010	-3.8	H14
Trail junction up East Fork Bear Creek	w	1.4	867.8	9530	-3.7	H14
Lake Italy Trail	w	1.2	869.0	9300	-2.1	H14
Old trail below Hilgard Creek	w	2.0	871.0	9040	-1.4	H14
Bear Ridge trail junction to Mono Hot Springs	w	1.6	872.6	9980	6.4	H15
Mono Creek	w	4.6	877.2	7850	-5.0	H15
Vermillion Valley Resort c/o Rancheria Garage Attn: (Your Name) PCT Hiker 62311 Huntington Lake Road Lakeshore, CA 93634 (559) 259-4000 Via UPS Only!	w,G,M,L, R: 6.00m W	0.0	877.2	7850	-5.0	H15
Junction with Mono Pass Trail	—	1.6	878.8	8270	2.8	H15
North Fork Mono Creek	w	1.4	880.2	8940	5.2	H15
Re-ford North Fork Mono Creek	w	1.2	881.4	9640	6.3	H15

CENTRAL CALIFORNIA

Landmark	Facilities	Diff	S->N	Elev	Gra	Map
Silver Pass	—	2.8	884.2	10900	4.9	H15
Goodale Pass Trail	w	1.2	885.4	10550	-3.2	H16
Cascade Valley Trail	w	2.5	887.9	9130	-6.2	H16
Tully Hole	w	1.1	889.0	9520	3.9	H16
Lake Virginia	w	1.9	890.9	10314	4.5	H16
Purple Lake	w	2.1	893.0	9900	-2.1	H16
Trail to Duck Lake	w	2.3	895.3	10150	1.2	H16
Deer Creek	w	5.5	900.8	9090	-2.1	H17
Upper Crater Meadow	—	2.0	902.8	8920	-0.9	H18
General Delivery Mammoth Lakes, CA 93546 (760) 934-2205	PO,w,G,M,L,r, R: 7.25m NE	0.0	902.8	8920	-0.9	H18
Last campsite before Reds Meadow	w	0.8	903.6	8660	-3.5	H18
Boundary Creek	w	2.3	905.9	7910	-3.5	H18
Abandoned stagecoach road	R	0.7	906.6	7700	-3.3	H18
Reds Meadow, few supplies	w,G,M,L: 0.30m N	0.0	906.6	7700	-3.3	H18
Reds Meadow, Rainbow Falls-Fish Valley-Cascade Valley Trail	—	0.2	906.8	7600	-5.4	H18
Trail junction by east boundary of Devils Postpile NM	—	0.5	907.3	7430	-3.7	H18
Old trans-Sierra Mammoth Trail	—	1.0	908.3	7710	3.0	H18
JMT and PCT diverge	—	0.6	908.9	7660	-0.9	H18
Minaret Creek	w	0.6	909.5	7590	-1.3	H18
Bridge across Middle Fork	—	1.4	910.9	7680	0.7	H18
Permanent stream along Middle Fork	w	1.0	911.9	7810	1.4	H19
Another stream	w	1.1	913.0	7910	1.0	H19
Junction after a small knoll	—	0.2	913.2	8000	4.9	H19
River Trail	—	0.5	913.7	8280	6.1	H19

CENTRAL CALIFORNIA

Landmark	Facilities	Diff	S->N	Elev	Gra	Map
Agnew Meadows Road	w,R	0.9	914.6	8360	1.0	H19
Ansel Adams Wilderness Boundary	w	2.8	917.4	9680	5.1	H19
Junction with trail over Agnew Pass	—	2.4	919.8	9710	0.1	H19
Middle Fork-Clark Lakes Trail	—	0.8	920.6	9500	-2.8	H20
De facto trail, pass a lakelet	w	0.3	920.9	9590	3.3	H20
River Trail	—	0.5	921.4	9560	-0.7	H20
Thousand Island Lake	w	1.0	922.4	9840	3.0	H20
Island Pass	—	1.8	924.2	10200	2.2	H20
Obscure junction to Davis Lake	—	1.0	925.2	9690	-5.5	H20
Rush Creek Trail	w	0.4	925.6	9600	-2.4	H20
Marie Lakes Trail	—	0.8	926.4	10030	5.8	H21
Donohue Pass	—	2.6	929.0	11056	4.3	H22
Lyell Fork crossing	w	1.8	930.8	10220	-5.0	H22
Another Lyell Fork crossing	w	0.8	931.6	9700	-7.1	H22
Lyell Fork base camp	w	1.4	933.0	9000	-5.4	H22
Junction to Vogelsang High Sierra Camp	w	2.8	935.8	8880	-0.5	H22
Rafferty Creek Trail	—	4.4	940.2	8710	-0.4	H23
Junction to Tuolumne Meadows Campground	—	0.7	940.9	8650	-0.9	H23
Dana Fork of the Tuolumne River	w	0.7	941.6	8690	0.6	H23
General Delivery Tuolumne Meadows, CA 95389 (209) 372-4475	PO,w,G,M,L,sh,r, R: 0.30m W	0.0	941.6	8690	0.6	H23
Tuolumne Lodge's road	R	0.3	941.9	8650	-1.4	H23
Highway 120	R	0.8	942.7	8595	-0.7	H23
Fork just beyond a minor gap	—	0.7	943.4	8590	-0.1	I1
Soda Springs area	—	0.1	943.5	8600	1.1	I1
Delaney Creek	w	0.8	944.3	8570	-0.4	I1

CENTRAL CALIFORNIA

Landmark	Facilities	Diff	S->N	Elev	Gra	Map
Young Lakes Trail	—	0.4	944.7	8650	2.2	I1
Bridge over Tuolumne River	w	2.7	947.4	8310	-1.4	I2
Junction to McGee Lake	—	1.1	948.5	7920	-3.9	I2
Glen Aulin, next to Conness Creek	w	0.2	948.7	7840	-4.3	I2
Forested gap along Cold Canyon creek	—	2.9	951.6	8800	3.6	I3
McCabe Lakes Trail	—	3.9	955.5	9080	0.8	I3
Virginia Canyon Trail	w	1.2	956.7	8540	-4.9	I3
Forested pass	—	2.2	958.9	9560	5.0	I3
Miller Lake	w	1.4	960.3	9490	-0.5	I3
Low gap	—	0.6	960.9	9680	3.4	I3
Matterhorn Canyon Trail	w	1.6	962.5	8510	-8.0	I3
Wilson Creek, last ford	w	3.3	965.8	9500	3.3	I4
Benson Pass	—	1.2	967.0	10140	5.8	I4
South shore on Smedberg Lake	w	1.9	968.9	9250	-5.1	I4
Well-defined gap	—	0.3	969.2	9340	3.3	I4
Meadowy junction to Rodgers Lake	—	0.7	969.9	9480	2.2	I4
Junction to Murdock Lake	—	0.3	970.2	9390	-3.3	I5
Ford of Smedberg Lake's outlet	w	0.8	971.0	8720	-9.1	I5
Benson Lake Trail Junction	—	2.1	973.1	7560	-6.0	I5
Wind-free, sparkling pond	w	2.1	975.2	8970	7.3	I5
Seavey Pass	w	0.6	975.8	9150	3.3	I5
Highest gap	—	0.2	976.0	9180	1.6	I5
Junction in Kerrick Canyon	w	0.5	976.5	8930	-5.4	I5
Lower Kerrick Canyon, Bear Valley Trail junction	w	3.7	980.2	7960	-2.8	I6
North to a shallow gap	—	1.4	981.6	8720	5.9	I6
Stubblefield Canyon creek	w	1.1	982.7	7740	-9.7	I6
Macomb Ridge pass	—	2.4	985.1	8910	5.3	I7

CENTRAL CALIFORNIA

Landmark	Facilities	Diff	S->N	Elev	Gra	Map
Tilden Lake Trail signed junction	w	1.0	986.1	8390	-5.7	I7
Wilma Lake or Wilmer Lake	w	1.5	987.6	7930	-3.3	I7
Junction with Jack Main Canyon Trail	w	0.3	987.9	7970	1.4	I7
Junction east to Tilden Lake	w	1.9	989.8	8160	1.1	I8
South end of Grace Meadow	w	3.7	993.5	8630	1.4	I8
First trail to Bond Pass	—	3.1	996.6	9280	2.3	I9
Dorothy Lake Pass	—	1.5	998.1	9550	2.0	I9
Lake Harriet	w	1.1	999.2	9210	-3.4	I9
Cascade Creek footbridge	w	0.7	999.9	9040	-2.6	I9
Junction to West Walker River Trail	w	0.6	1000.5	9000	-0.7	I9
Junction just past a creek after 3 ponds	w	0.9	1001.4	9320	3.9	I9
West Fork West Walker River Trail	w	2.0	1003.4	8670	-3.5	I9
West Fork West Walker River bridge, junction by Lower Long Lake	w	0.2	1003.6	8610	-3.3	I9
Another creek	w	1.6	1005.2	8610	0.0	I9
Kennedy Canyon creek	w	1.9	1007.1	9060	2.6	I10
Closed jeep road	R	1.2	1008.3	9670	5.5	I10
Leave jeep road at a switchback	R	1.9	1010.2	10580	5.2	I10
Sierra crest	—	2.3	1012.5	10640	0.3	I10
Ridge, highest point after Donohue Pass	—	0.7	1013.2	10880	3.7	I10
Notch on a steep wall	—	0.7	1013.9	10780	-1.6	I10
Another crest crossing	—	0.8	1014.7	10780	0.0	I10
Another crest crossing	—	1.2	1015.9	10870	0.8	I10
First creek since Kennedy Canyon	w	1.7	1017.6	9820	-6.7	I10
Sonora Pass (Highway 108)	R	0.7	1018.3	9620	-3.1	I10
Trailhead-parking spur	—	0.2	1018.5	9610	-0.5	J1

CENTRAL CALIFORNIA

Landmark	Facilities	Diff	S->N	Elev	Gra	Map
Start switchback	—	1.7	1020.2	10080	3.0	J1
County-line ridge	—	0.7	1020.9	10420	5.3	J1
Top the Sierra crest at a saddle	—	0.3	1021.2	10500	2.9	J1
Junction atop Wolf Creek Lake saddle to Wolf Creek Lake	w: 0.33m S	1.2	1022.4	10250	-2.3	J1
East Carson River Trail, descend to a small flat	w	5.2	1027.6	8100	-4.5	J2
Prominent crest saddle, junction to Boulder Lake	—	3.1	1030.7	8590	1.7	J2
Boulder Creek	w	1.6	1032.3	8600	0.1	J2
Descend to a saddle by Golden Lake	—	2.3	1034.6	9170	2.7	J3
Junction with Paradise Valley and Golden Canyon Trails	—	1.2	1035.8	9170	0.0	J3
Saddle with view of Peak 9500	—	0.7	1036.5	9340	2.6	J3
Another saddle after Murray Canyon	—	1.5	1038.0	9080	-1.9	J3
East Fork of Wolf Creek	w	2.0	1040.0	8320	-4.1	J3
Middle Fork of Wolf Creek	w	0.4	1040.4	8310	-0.3	J3
Multi-branched West Fork	w	0.5	1040.9	8400	2.0	J3
Sierra Nevada Crest	—	0.8	1041.7	8800	5.4	J3
Wolf Creek Pass	w	1.0	1042.7	8410	-4.2	J3
Junction by a gully to Asa Lake	—	0.3	1043.0	8480	2.5	J3
Asa Lake's outlet creek	w	0.2	1043.2	8520	2.2	J3
Saddle	—	1.7	1044.9	9330	5.2	J4
Junction with Noble Canyon Trail	—	0.6	1045.5	9110	-4.0	J4
Noble Lake outlet creek	w	0.6	1046.1	8900	-3.8	J4
Junction with northern part of Noble Canyon Trail	w	0.9	1047.0	8360	-6.5	J4
Highway 4 near Ebbetts Pass	R	2.9	1049.9	8700	1.3	J4
Sherrold Lake	w	0.6	1050.5	8760	1.1	J4

CENTRAL CALIFORNIA

Landmark	Facilities	Diff	S->N	Elev	Gra	Map
Raymond Meadows Creek	w	3.4	1053.9	8640	-0.4	J5
Eagle Creek	w	1.1	1055.0	8460	-1.8	J5
Deep crest saddle	—	1.3	1056.3	8510	0.4	J5
Pennsylvania Creek	w	0.6	1056.9	8140	-6.7	J5
Sagebrush saddle	—	1.0	1057.9	8660	5.7	J5
Side Trail to Raymond Lake	—	1.5	1059.4	8640	-0.1	J5
Raymond Lake Creek	w	1.0	1060.4	8150	-5.3	J5
Conspicuous saddle	—	0.8	1061.2	8230	1.1	J5
Pleasant Valley Trail 008	—	0.6	1061.8	7820	-7.4	J5
Tributary of Pleasant Valley Creek	w	0.4	1062.2	7860	1.1	J5
Saddle leaving the eastern part of Mokelumne Wilderness	—	0.5	1062.7	8200	7.4	J5
Spur trail to Wet Meadows Trailhead	—	0.1	1062.8	8160	-4.3	J5
Reach a road	R	1.5	1064.3	7900	-1.9	J5
Car-camping site	w	0.6	1064.9	7840	-1.1	J5
Blue Lakes Road	R	2.7	1067.6	8090	1.0	J6
Saddle southeast of The Nipple	—	2.4	1070.0	8830	3.3	J6
Lost Lakes spur road	w,R	1.8	1071.8	8660	-1.0	J6
Muddy pond	—	1.6	1073.4	8830	1.2	J6
Summit City Canyon Trail 18E07	—	0.2	1073.6	8880	2.7	J7
Circles a third tiny pond	w	0.8	1074.4	8630	-3.4	J7
Rejoin TYT near Frog Lake, junction to Winnemucca Lake	w	3.1	1077.5	8860	0.8	J7
Junction south of Frog Lake	w	0.1	1077.6	8870	1.1	J7
Highway 88, south end of a long parking lot with Carson Pass markers	R	1.1	1078.7	8580	-2.9	J8
Flat parking area	—	0.2	1078.9	8550	-1.6	J8
Pond-blessed saddle	w	1.4	1080.3	8800	1.9	J8

CENTRAL CALIFORNIA

Landmark	Facilities	Diff	S->N	Elev	Gra	Map
Campsite by infant Upper Truckee River	w	0.8	1081.1	8460	-4.6	J8
Branch right after 2 cabins	w	0.7	1081.8	8380	-1.2	J8
Upper Truckee River	w	0.6	1082.4	8310	-1.3	J8
Second trail from Schneider Camp	—	1.5	1083.9	8650	2.5	J8
Showers Lake	w	0.1	1084.0	8620	-3.3	J8
Junction with Trail 17E16	—	1.9	1085.9	8960	1.9	J9
Shallow gap	—	0.2	1086.1	8890	-3.8	J9
Saddle junction with Sayles Canyon Trail 17E14	—	1.4	1087.5	8630	-2.0	J9
Bryan Meadow	w	0.9	1088.4	8540	-1.1	J9
Second creek crossing by Benwood Meadow	w	1.1	1089.5	8340	-2.0	J9
Junction after Benwood Meadow to alternate route to Echo Lake Resort	—	1.8	1091.3	7475	-5.2	J9
Road 1N03	R	1.0	1092.3	7390	-0.9	J9
Highway 50	R	0.7	1093.0	7220	-2.6	J9
Lake of the Sky Outfitters Attn: (Your Name) PCT Hiker 1023 Emerald Bay Road South Lake Tahoe, CA 96150 (530) 541-1027 Open 7 days, call to check	w,G,M,L,sh,r, R: 9.50m NE	0.0	1093.0	7220	-2.6	J9
General Delivery South Lake Tahoe, CA 96150 (530) 541-4365	PO,w,G,M,L,sh, R: 9.70m NE	0.0	1093.0	7220	-2.6	J9
Echo Lake Resort		1.3	1094.3	7525	2.5	J9
Lower Echo Lake	w	0.2	1094.5	7414	-6.0	J9
General Delivery Echo Lake, CA 95721 (530) 659-7207	PO,w,G,M,L,r,R	0.0	1094.5	7414	-6.0	J9
Junction to a saddle and Triangle Lake	—	3.1	1097.6	7700	1.0	K2

CENTRAL CALIFORNIA

Landmark	Facilities	Diff	S->N	Elev	Gra	Map
Another trail junction	—	0.5	1098.1	7865	3.6	K2
Lateral trail above Triangle Lake	—	0.7	1098.8	8250	6.0	K2
North-facing-slope junction with second trail to Lake of the Woods	—	0.5	1099.3	8350	2.2	K2
Past a trail above Lake Margery	—	0.5	1099.8	8340	-0.2	K2
Past a trail going to Lake Margery	—	0.2	1100.0	8310	-1.6	K2
Junction above Lake Aloha	—	0.6	1100.6	8140	-3.1	K2
Reach a gully	w	0.5	1101.1	8190	1.1	K2
Junction with Rubicon River Trail	w	0.9	1102.0	8120	-0.8	K2
Heather Lake's northwest shore	w	0.7	1102.7	7900	-3.4	K2
Cross Susie Lake outlet creek	w	1.1	1103.8	7790	-1.1	K2
Swampy meadow where the trail forks	—	0.6	1104.4	7680	-2.0	K2
Intersection down to Fallen Leaf area	—	0.5	1104.9	7940	5.7	K2
Junction with Trail 17E09 to Gilmore Lake	w	0.6	1105.5	8290	6.3	K2
Dicks Pass	—	2.3	1107.8	9380	5.1	K2
Descend to a rocky saddle, reach a junction to Eagle Falls Picnic Area	—	1.7	1109.5	8500	-5.6	K2
Reach a spur trail to Dicks Lake	—	0.2	1109.7	8450	-2.7	K2
Trail junction above Middle Velma Lake	—	1.9	1111.6	7965	-2.8	K3
Trail descending west to Camper Flat	—	0.3	1111.9	7940	-0.9	K3
Junction where PCT and TYT splits	—	1.1	1113.0	8090	1.5	K3
Seasonal Phipps Creek	w	1.5	1114.5	7620	-3.4	K3
High point	—	2.0	1116.5	8120	2.7	K3
Junction to Lake Genevieve	—	0.9	1117.4	7880	-2.9	K4
Jeep road atop a forested saddle	R	2.7	1120.1	7570	-1.2	K4

CENTRAL CALIFORNIA

Landmark	Facilities	Diff	S->N	Elev	Gra	Map
Richardson Lake's northwest corner	w	0.5	1120.6	7400	-3.7	K4
Lightly used road by Miller Creek	w,R	1.7	1122.3	7020	-2.4	K4
McKinney-Rubicon Springs Road	R	0.2	1122.5	7000	-1.1	K4
Bear lake road	R	1.9	1124.4	7120	0.7	K5
Forest Route 3 near Barker Pass	—	2.4	1126.8	7650	2.4	K5
General Delivery Tahoe City, CA 96145 (530) 583-6563	PO,w,G,M,L, R: 12.00m NE	0.0	1126.8	7650	2.4	K5
Saddle after a spring-fed gullly	—	1.6	1128.4	8240	4.0	K5
North Fork Blackwood Creek campsites	w	0.8	1129.2	7960	-3.8	K5
Low knoll with excellent views	—	2.4	1131.6	8370	1.9	K5
PCT and Tahoe Rim Trail splits	—	0.2	1131.8	8430	3.3	K5
Ward Peak maintenance road	R	3.3	1135.1	8470	0.1	K6
Five Lakes Creek, Trail 16E04	w	3.1	1138.2	7430	-3.6	K6
Whiskey Creek Trail 16E06	—	1.4	1139.6	7170	-2.0	K6
Tevis Cup Trail	—	2.1	1141.7	7915	3.9	K6
Headwaters of Middle Fork American River	w	0.6	1142.3	8140	4.1	K7
Minor gap just outside of Granite Chief Wilderness	—	0.7	1143.0	8550	6.4	K7
Squaw Creek	w	0.4	1143.4	8270	-7.6	K7
Water Alert (↓): 15.5m						
Granite Chief Trail 15E23 to Squaw Valley	—	1.1	1144.5	8170	-1.0	K7
Painted Rock Trail 15E06	—	1.5	1146.0	7550	-4.5	K7
Tinker Knob saddle	—	2.2	1148.2	8590	5.1	K7
Sierra crest	—	0.3	1148.5	8760	6.2	K7
Saddle north of Anderson Peak	—	1.8	1150.3	8230	-3.2	K8
Round Peak 8374 to a shallower saddle	—	0.5	1150.8	8170	-1.3	K8

CENTRAL CALIFORNIA

Landmark	Facilities	Diff	S->N	Elev	Gra	Map
Roller Pass	—	2.8	1153.6	7900	-1.0	K8
South end of Mt. Judah Loop	—	0.1	1153.7	7870	-3.3	K8
Cross one-lane road	R	0.7	1154.4	7520	-5.4	K8
North end of Mt. Judah Loop	—	0.2	1154.6	7560	2.2	K8
Road junction to Lake Mary homesites	R	1.0	1155.6	7060	-5.4	K8
Old Highway 40 near Donner Pass	R	0.2	1155.8	7090	1.6	K8
General Delivery Soda Springs, CA 95728 (530) 426-3082	PO,w,G,M,r, R: 3.20m W	0.0	1155.8	7090	1.6	K8
Parking, junction .25 mile south of Interstate 80	w: 0.12m N	3.0	1158.8	7190	0.4	K8
Water Alert (↑): 15.4m						
Junction by a lakelet's west shore	w	0.9	1159.7	7230	0.5	L1
Northwest to a road	R	1.0	1160.7	7440	2.3	L1
Castle Pass	—	1.4	1162.1	7910	3.6	L1
Peter Grubb Hut	w	0.9	1163.0	7820	-1.1	L1
Old jeep road	R	2.2	1165.2	8270	2.2	L2
Magonigal Camp jeep road	w,R	1.9	1167.1	7580	-3.9	L2
Reach a knoll	—	1.1	1168.2	8120	5.3	L2
Mt. Lola Trail Junction	—	1.1	1169.3	7620	-4.9	L2
White Rock Creek	w	0.1	1169.4	7630	1.1	L2
Road 19N11A	R	0.7	1170.1	7760	2.0	L2
Saddle over Jackson Meadow Reservoir	—	0.8	1170.9	8140	5.2	L2
Cross a road on a viewless saddle	R	0.7	1171.6	8060	-1.2	L3
Ridge saddle at the head of Bear Valley	—	1.0	1172.6	7830	-2.5	L3
Tahoe N.F. Road 86, Meadow Lake Road 19N11	w,R	2.1	1174.7	7530	-1.6	L3
Climbs to a ridge	—	1.1	1175.8	8000	4.6	L3

CENTRAL CALIFORNIA

Landmark	Facilities	Diff	S->N	Elev	Gra	Map
Logging road	R	2.1	1177.9	7640	-1.9	L3
Descend to a creek	w	3.6	1181.5	7330	-0.9	L3
Minor saddle	—	0.4	1181.9	7135	-5.3	L4
Cross another good road	R	2.3	1184.2	6740	-1.9	L4
Junction southeast of Pass Creek Loop Road	w,R	1.7	1185.9	6170	-3.6	L5
Tahoe N. F. Road 07 near Jackson Meadow Reservoir	w,R: 0.25m W	0.4	1186.3	6200	0.8	L5
Minor saddle	—	0.8	1187.1	6450	3.4	L5
First (southern) Milton Creek crossing	w	5.5	1192.6	5240	-2.4	L5
Bridge over Milton Creek	w	0.8	1193.4	4990	-3.4	L5
Northward down to closed road to Wild Plum Campground	R	1.2	1194.6	4810	-1.6	L6
Bridge over Haypress Creek	w	0.3	1194.9	4720	-3.3	L6
1001 Mine Creek	—	0.4	1195.3	4800	2.2	L6
Bridge over North Yuba River	w	1.9	1197.2	4600	-1.1	L6
Highway 49 near Sierra City	R	0.4	1197.6	4570	-0.8	L6
General Delivery Sierra City, CA 96125 (530) 862-1152	PO,w,G,M,L,r, R: 1.50m SW	0.0	1197.6	4570	-0.8	M1
Switchback up to a flume	w: 0.10m N	2.7	1200.3	5720	4.6	M1
Switchback tops off on a ridge	—	0.7	1201.0	6070	5.4	M1
Sierra Buttes jeep trail	—	3.8	1204.8	7150	3.1	M1
Ridgecrest trail junction	—	1.1	1205.9	7350	2.0	M1
Down to a gap on a jeep road	R	0.9	1206.8	7010	-4.1	M1
Packer Lake saddle	—	0.6	1207.4	7020	0.2	M1
Jeep road to Deer Lake	R	2.8	1210.2	7430	1.6	M2
Junction to Trail 12E02	—	0.3	1210.5	7370	-2.2	M2
Summit Lake Road Junction	w,R: 0.10m SW	1.3	1211.8	7050	-2.7	M2

CENTRAL CALIFORNIA

Landmark	Facilities	Diff	S->N	Elev	Gra	Map
Jeep road cuts northeast across the crest	R	1.3	1213.1	7290	2.0	M2
Reach a junction to Oakland Pond	—	0.9	1214.0	7355	0.8	M2
County-line crest saddle with a diminutive pond	w: 0.12m E	2.3	1216.3	7050	-1.4	M2
Cross a jeep road, twice almost touching it	R	1.3	1217.6	7330	2.3	M3
Down to a saddle	—	1.8	1219.4	6630	-4.2	M3
The "A" Tree, focal point for 5 roads	w,R	0.5	1219.9	6550	-1.7	M3
Rise to a saddle after diverging from Cowell Mine Road	R	1.1	1221.0	6920	3.7	M3
Saddle south end of McRae Ridge	—	0.8	1221.8	7380	6.3	M3
Descend to a spot near some campsites	w	3.2	1225.0	6150	-4.2	M3
Leave Section 30 and West Branch Nelson Creek	w	1.3	1226.3	5790	-3.0	M4
Johnsville-Gibsonville Road	R	1.2	1227.5	6065	2.5	M4
South end of Bunker Hill Ridge	—	3.0	1230.5	6750	2.5	M4
Small, unnamed lake just west of the trail below Bunker Hill Ridge	w	1.5	1232.0	6810	0.4	M4
Second saddle next to seasonal spring	w	0.7	1232.7	6700	-1.7	M4
Forested slopes to a road	R	1.9	1234.6	6680	-0.1	M5
Quincy-LaPorte Road, continue on a level spur road out to a saddle	w,R: 0.25m SE	1.0	1235.6	6474	-2.2	M5
Cross Road 22N60 at a saddle	R	0.9	1236.5	6510	0.4	M5
Recross Road 22N60 at another saddle	R	1.9	1238.4	5900	-3.5	M5
Cross Bear Wallow Trail at a jeep road	w,R: 0.50m S	1.4	1239.8	5755	-1.1	M6
Chimney Rock	—	1.0	1240.8	6000	2.7	M6
Black Rock Creek Road 22N56 at a saddle	w,R: 0.25m S	2.1	1242.9	5460	-2.8	M6

CENTRAL CALIFORNIA

Landmark	Facilities	Diff	S->N	Elev	Gra	Map
Junction to Fowler Lake	—	1.2	1244.1	5500	0.4	M6
Reach a second road	R	0.3	1244.4	5280	-8.0	M6
Sawmill Tom Creek Road 23N65Y	R	1.0	1245.4	5060	-2.4	M6
Almost touch the road at a saddle	R	1.8	1247.2	4910	-0.9	M7
Cross road known as Dogwood Creek Road, Butte Road, and Road 23N29X	R	1.6	1248.8	4240	-4.5	M7
Switchback to a delicious spring	w	2.3	1251.1	3180	-5.0	M7
Middle Fork Feather River	w	0.4	1251.5	2900	-7.6	M7
Deadman Spring saddle	—	1.4	1252.9	3590	5.4	M7
Bear Creek	w	2.1	1255.0	3240	-1.8	M7
Switchback to another ridge	—	2.5	1257.5	4250	4.4	M7
Seasonal spring	w	2.3	1259.8	5350	5.2	M8
Sunny crest saddle	—	1.4	1261.2	5750	3.1	M8
Seasonal Spring just before Lookout Tower	w	0.3	1261.5	5870	4.3	M8
Lookout Rock	—	0.3	1261.8	5955	3.1	M8
Road 23N19	R	0.7	1262.5	5870	-1.3	M8
Road branching north	R	1.3	1263.8	5880	0.1	M9
Big Creek Road 33N56	w,R	1.6	1265.4	5505	-2.5	M9
Final water supply, a creeklet	w	2.4	1267.8	5520	0.1	M9
Water Alert (↓): 12.4m						
Bucks Summit	—	2.4	1270.2	5531	0.0	M9
Path on a shady left where road turns counterclockwise	R	2.6	1272.8	6550	4.3	M10
Shallow saddle, meet Spanish Peak road again	R	1.6	1274.4	6920	2.5	M10
Trail junction to Gold Lake Trail	—	1.4	1275.8	6870	-0.4	M10
Cross a jeep road	R	1.2	1277.0	6880	0.1	M10
Descend to a forested saddle	—	1.0	1278.0	6710	-1.8	M10

Central California

CENTRAL CALIFORNIA

Landmark	Facilities	Diff	S->N	Elev	Gra	Map
Clear Creek	w	2.2	1280.2	6190	-2.6	M11
Water Alert (↑): 12.4m						
Old California Riding and Hiking Trail by a pond	w	0.5	1280.7	6240	1.1	M11
Junction with CRHT that descends to Three Lakes	—	1.0	1281.7	6270	0.3	M11
Shady bend on an old fire road	R	0.4	1282.1	6260	-0.3	M11
Road dead-ends where Belden Trail of PCT begins	R	1.8	1283.9	5900	-2.2	M11
Western Pacific's 2 railroad tracks	—	4.7	1288.6	2310	-8.3	M11
Belden Town	—	0.6	1289.2	2310	0.0	M11
Highway 70 at Belden Town bridge	R	0.1	1289.3	2330	2.2	M11
Belden Town Resort and Lodge 14785 Belden Town Road Belden, CA 95915 (530) 283-9662	w,G,M,L,sh	0.0	1289.3	2330	2.2	M11
Caribou Crossroads Campground Caribou Road Belden, CA 95915 (530) 283-1384	w,G,M,sh, R: 1.80m NW	0.0	1289.3	2330	2.2	M11
General Delivery Belden, CA 95915 (530) 533-8206	PO,w,r,R: 0.90m SW	0.0	1289.3	2330	2.2	M11

Central California

NORTHERN CALIFORNIA

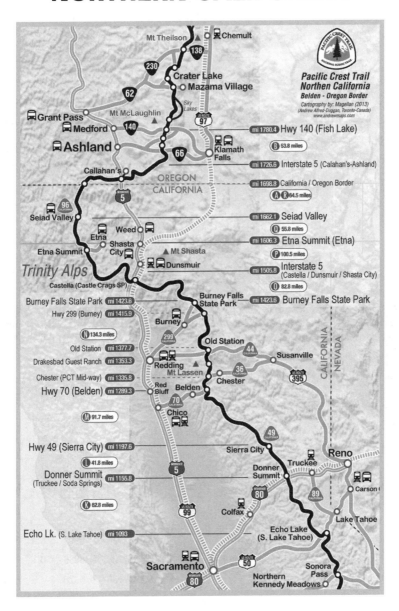

Mt Theilson ▲ ○ 🚌🚉 Chemult
138
230
Crater Lake
○ Mazama Village
62
Sky Lakes
Grant Pass 🚌
Mt McLaughlin ▲
🚌 Medford ○ 140
Ashland ○
66
Callahan's ○
OREGON
CALIFORNIA
5
96
Seiad Valley
Weed ○ 🚌
Etna
Shasta City 🚌
Etna Summit ○
▲ Mt Shasta
Trinity Alps
○ 🚌🚉 Dunsmuir
Castella (Castle Crags SP) ○
Burney Falls State Park mi 1423.6
Hwy 299 (Burney) mi 1415.9
🚌 Burney
Burney Falls State Park
N 134.3 miles
Old Station mi 1377.7
Old Station
Drakesbad Guest Ranch mi 1353.3
299
Redding 🚌🚉
44
Susanville
Mt Lassen ▲
36
Chester (PCT Mid-way) mi 1335.8
Red Bluff ○ Belden
Chester
395
Hwy 70 (Belden) mi 1289.3
70
○ Chico 🚌🚉
M 91.7 miles
49
Hwy 49 (Sierra City) mi 1197.6
Sierra City
Truckee Reno
L 41.8 miles
5
Donner Summit
🚌🚉
Donner Summit
(Truckee / Soda Springs) mi 1155.8
80
89
○ Carson
K 62.8 miles
99
Colfax ○ 🚌
Lake Tahoe
Echo Lk. (S. Lake Tahoe) mi 1093
Echo Lake
(S. Lake Tahoe)
🚌🚉
Sacramento
50
Sonora Pass ○
80
Northern Kennedy Meadows ○

Pacific Crest Trail
Northen California
Belden - Oregon Border
Cartography by: Magellan (2013)
(Andrew Alfred-Duggan, Toronto-Canada)
www.andrewmaps.com

mi 1780.4 Hwy 140 (Fish Lake)
B 53.8 miles
mi 1726.6 Interstate 5 (Calahan's-Ashland)
mi 1698.8 California / Oregon Border
A R 64.5 miles
mi 1662.1 Seiad Valley
Q 55.8 miles
mi 1606.3 Etna Summit (Etna)
P 100.5 miles
mi 1505.8 Interstate 5
(Castella / Dunsmuir / Shasta City)
O 82.8 miles
mi 1423.6 Burney Falls State Park

CALIFORNIA
NEVADA

NORTHERN CALIFORNIA

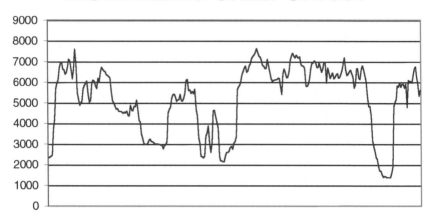

**Elevation Profile for Northern California
From Belden to California-Oregon Border**

Section Total Mileage: 408.2 miles

Landmark	Facilities	Diff	S->N	Elev	Gra	Map
Bridge over Indian Creek	w	1.1	1290.4	2370	0.4	N1
Meet a trail after turning west	—	0.3	1290.7	2400	1.1	N1
Junction to an old road	R	0.6	1291.3	2470	1.3	N1
Williams Cabin Flat, small cabin on a white-fir-shaded flat	w	4.2	1295.5	3700	3.2	N1
Myrtle Flat Camp	w	0.9	1296.4	4180	5.8	N2
Creek fed by Poison Spring	w	3.8	1300.2	5650	4.2	N3
Junction with an old road	R	0.4	1300.6	5920	7.3	N3
Leave old road, forking right	R	0.5	1301.1	6100	3.9	N3
Vicinity of Poison Spring headwater	w	1.2	1302.3	6680	5.3	N3
Wide lumber road	R	0.4	1302.7	6900	6.0	N3
Spring	w	1.0	1303.7	6960	0.7	N3
Spur ridge to a roadend	R	1.5	1305.2	6620	-2.5	N3

NORTHERN CALIFORNIA

Landmark	Facilities	Diff	S->N	Elev	Gra	Map
Another PCT trail segment	—	0.7	1305.9	6610	-0.2	N4
Road 26N02	R	1.0	1306.9	6380	-2.5	N4
Humbug Road 27N01 at Cold Springs	w,R	1.7	1308.6	6450	0.4	N4
Past second road	R	0.7	1309.3	6710	4.0	N4
Pond west of the trail	w	1.6	1310.9	7100	2.6	N4
North end to a jeep road that levels east to Lost Lake	R	0.9	1311.8	7000	-1.2	N4
Humboldt Road at Humboldt Summit	R	3.6	1315.4	6610	-1.2	N5
Descend lowest saddle	—	3.9	1319.3	6155	-1.3	N5
Carter Meadow Trail junction	w: 0.50m N	2.3	1321.6	6600	2.1	N5
Junction to Butt Mountain summit	—	3.7	1325.3	7590	2.9	N5
Shallow gully	—	2.6	1327.9	6920	-2.8	N6
Recross Soldier Creek Springs	w	4.2	1332.1	5480	-3.7	N7
Road after private property	R	1.5	1333.6	5150	-2.4	N7
Grassy trough	—	0.7	1334.3	4870	-4.3	N7
Highway 36	R	1.5	1335.8	4990	0.9	N7
General Delivery Chester, CA 96020 (530) 258-4184	PO,w,G,M,L,sh, R: 8.00m NE	0.0	1335.8	4990	0.9	N7
Marian Creek, dry most of summer	w	1.6	1337.4	5060	0.5	N7
Stover Camp, spring	w	1.6	1339.0	5660	4.1	N7
Cross a major road	R	1.1	1340.1	5810	1.5	N7
County-line crest	—	1.4	1341.5	5920	0.9	N7
North Stover Mountain	—	0.7	1342.2	6050	2.0	N7
Major logging road on a ridge	R	1.6	1343.8	5400	-4.4	N8
Bridge over North Fork Feather River	w	1.0	1344.8	5020	-4.1	N8
Chester-Childs Meadows Road	R	0.9	1345.7	5110	1.1	N8

NORTHERN CALIFORNIA

Landmark	Facilities	Diff	S->N	Elev	Gra	Map
Descend northwest to an abandoned road	R	4.1	1349.8	5960	2.3	N8
Swampy Little Willow Lake	w	0.7	1350.5	6100	2.2	N8
Junction to Terminal Geyser	—	1.0	1351.5	6030	-0.8	N8
Trail to Drakesbad Guest Ranch	—	1.8	1353.3	5800	-1.4	N9
Drakesbad Guest Ranch (866) 999-0914	w,M,L: 0.30m W	0.0	1353.3	5800	-1.4	N9
Warner Valley Campground	w	0.9	1354.2	5670	-1.6	N9
Junction to Bench Lake	—	1.0	1355.2	6180	5.5	N9
Campsites, junction to Summit Lake	w	1.4	1356.6	5990	-1.5	N9
Junction to Horseshoe Lake	w	2.5	1359.1	6470	2.1	N9
Second junction that meets the first junction to Horseshoe Lake	—	1,3	1360.4	6710	2.0	N9
Swan Lake outlet creek	w	0.5	1360.9	6620	-2.0	N9
Lower Twin Lake, south end	w	0.5	1361.4	6540	-1.7	N10
Lower Twin Lake, north end	w	0.4	1361.8	6545	0.1	N10
Trail descending left	—	0.4	1362.2	6520	-0.7	N10
Nobles Trail	—	2.6	1364.8	6354	-0.7	N10
Opening with view of Soap Lake	—	1.0	1365.8	6320	-0.4	N10
East end of Badger Flat	w	1.6	1367.4	6270	-0.3	N10
Junction to a horse camp, park's north boundary	—	2.1	1369.5	6200	-0.4	N11
Plantation Loop Road	R	1.5	1371.0	5560	-4.6	N11
East-west road	R	1.7	1372.7	5090	-3.0	N11
Western arm of the Plantation Loop Road	w,R	0.7	1373.4	4980	-1.7	N12
Road 32N12	R	1.0	1374.4	4830	-1.6	N12
Cross a road	R	1.4	1375.8	4690	-1.1	N12
Atop a faulted escarpment	—	0.9	1376.7	4720	0.4	N12
North-trending road	R	0.8	1377.5	4590	-1.8	N12

NORTHERN CALIFORNIA

Landmark	Facilities	Diff	S->N	Elev	Gra	Map
Gate across the road to Hat Creek Resort	R	0.2	1377.7	4580	-0.5	N12
General Delivery Old Station, CA 96071 (530) 335-7191	PO,w,G,M,L,sh,r, R: 0.30m N	0.0	1377.7	4580	-0.5	N12
Road 32N20	R	0.5	1378.2	4545	-0.8	N13
Road 32N99	R	0.7	1378.9	4480	-1.0	N13
Another crossing of Road 32N99	R	0.3	1379.2	4540	2.2	N13
Trail fork to Hat Creek Campground	—	0.4	1379.6	4500	-1.1	N13
Road 33N22	R	1.3	1380.9	4590	0.8	N13
Cross Highway 44 near Subway Cave	w,R: 0.25m W	0.9	1381.8	4365	-2.7	N13
Water Alert (↓): 29.4m						
Old Highway 44	R	1.4	1383.2	4360	0.0	N13
Highway 44 trailhead	R	1.5	1384.7	4870	3.7	N13
Cross usually dry creek gully	—	1.8	1386.5	4640	-1.4	N13
Another dry creek gully	—	0.9	1387.4	4600	-0.5	N14
Shallow depression	—	1.6	1389.0	4820	1.5	N14
Another dry creek gully	—	2.1	1391.1	4810	-0.1	N14
Hat Creek Rim Fire Lookout site	—	4.7	1395.8	5122	0.7	N14
Road 22	R	2.8	1398.6	4660	-1.8	N15
Down to a small reservoir, polluted	—	1.9	1400.5	4140	-3.0	N15
Closed gate below Road 36N18	R	3.1	1403.6	4030	-0.4	N16
Cross Cassel-Fall River Mills Road	R	3.8	1407.4	3480	-1.6	N17
Cross Conrad Ranch Road	R	2.1	1409.5	3270	-1.1	N17
Road above Rock Spring Creek	w,R	1.7	1411.2	3025	-1.6	N18
Water Alert (↓): 12.5m						
Water Alert (↑): 29.7m						
PG&E road south to Cassel	R	0.5	1411.7	2990	-0.8	N18

NORTHERN CALIFORNIA

Landmark	Facilities	Diff	S->N	Elev	Gra	Map
General Delivery Cassel, CA 96016 (530) 335-3100	PO,w,G,r, R: 1.50m SW	0.0	1411.7	2990	-0.8	N18
Crystal Lake State Fish Hatchery road	R	0.1	1411.8	3000	1.1	N18
Cross a jeep road	R	1.5	1413.3	3150	1.1	N18
Another jeep road	R	1.8	1415.1	3240	0.5	N18
Highway 299	R	0.8	1415.9	3110	-1.8	N18
General Delivery Burney, CA 96013 (530) 335-5430	PO,w,G,M,L, R: 7.00m SW	0.0	1415.9	3110	-1.8	N18
Slant across a major straight road	R	2.3	1418.2	3070	-0.2	N18
South edge of Arkright Flat	—	1.3	1419.5	2995	-0.6	N18
Cross a nearby road	R	0.4	1419.9	3005	0.3	N19
Rim of Lake Road	R	1.2	1421.1	3010	0.0	N19
Highway 89	R	1.5	1422.6	2995	-0.1	N19
Large backpacker's camp	—	0.4	1423.0	2970	-0.7	N19
Burney Falls, broad path to a parking area on Clark Creek Road	—	0.6	1423.6	2950	-0.4	N19
PCT Hikers Recreation Resource Mgmt Attn: (Your Name) PCT Hiker 24900 Highway 89 Burney, CA 96013 (530) 335-5713	w,G,M,sh,r, R: 0.10m E	0.0	1423.6	2950	-0.4	N19
Water Alert (↑): 12.4m						
Lake Britton's dam	—	1.9	1425.5	2760	-1.1	O1
Meet a jeep road	R	2.9	1428.4	2930	0.6	O2
Rock Creek	w	0.6	1429.0	2980	0.9	O2
Road 37N02	R	0.4	1429.4	3100	3.3	O2
Cross a road	R	4.3	1433.7	4480	3.5	O3
Old clearcut	—	1.4	1435.1	4660	1.4	O3
Peavine Creek	w	2.6	1437.7	4760	0.4	O3

NORTHERN CALIFORNIA

Landmark	Facilities	Diff	S->N	Elev	Gra	Map
Crackling powerlines	—	1.6	1439.3	5200	3.0	03
Road junction at south base of Red Mountain	R	1.2	1440.5	5380	1.6	03
Road 38N10	R	0.8	1441.3	5410	0.4	03
Another spur road	R	0.7	1442.0	5290	-1.9	04
Junction of 2 roads to Deadman Creek	w,R: 0.50m E	2.1	1444.1	5060	-1.2	04
Road 38N10	R	0.2	1444.3	5140	4.3	04
Descend to a logging road	R	1.4	1445.7	5150	0.1	04
Descend to a spot with panoramic view	—	1.8	1447.5	5390	1.4	04
Cross a descending road down to a pond	w,R: 0.50m SE	2.2	1449.7	5110	-1.4	04
Back to Road 38N10, just before Bartle Gap	w,R: 0.15m N	1.6	1451.3	5070	-0.3	04
Cross Road 39N90	R	0.4	1451.7	5190	3.3	04
Springs at Moosehead Creek's headwaters	w	1.3	1453.0	5440	2.1	05
Rocky point with a view	—	2.3	1455.3	6080	3.0	05
Cross Road 38N10	R	1.4	1456.7	6120	0.3	05
Tate Creek, resume at a junction with Road 38N10	w,R: 0.50m N	1.1	1457.8	5580	-5.3	05
Recross Road 38N10	R	1.5	1459.3	5610	0.2	06
Alder Creek Trail	w: 0.33m N	1.1	1460.4	5440	-1.7	06
Grizzly Peak Road before Pigeon Hill	R	2.1	1462.5	5540	0.5	06
Recross Grizzly Peak Road	R	0.6	1463.1	5420	-2.2	06
South ridge of Grizzly Peak Lookout road	R	2.6	1465.7	5640	0.9	06
Deer Creek	w	2.1	1467.8	4700	-4.9	07
Side canyon with refreshing creek	w	1.4	1469.2	4360	-2.6	07
Butcherknife Creek	w	3.2	1472.4	3300	-3.6	07

NORTHERN CALIFORNIA

Landmark	Facilities	Diff	S->N	Elev	Gra	Map
Dry Doodlebug Gulch	—	2.1	1474.5	3000	-1.6	07
McCloud-Big Bend Road	w,R	1.3	1475.8	2404	-5.0	07
Ash Camp	w	0.2	1476.0	2390	-0.8	08
Fitzhugh Gulch Creek	w	2.1	1478.1	2320	-0.4	08
Ah-Di-Na Campround road, Road 38N53	R	0.4	1478.5	2400	2.2	08
Bald Mountain Road	R	3.1	1481.6	3380	3.4	08
Climb to another road	R	0.8	1482.4	3520	1.9	08
Top a ridge saddle	—	1.9	1484.3	3880	2.1	08
Trough Creek	w	2.1	1486.4	3030	-4.4	09
Squaw Valley Creek	w	3.2	1489.6	2580	-1.5	09
Southwest to a deep saddle	—	0.9	1490.5	3059	5.8	09
Girard Ridge Road	R	4.8	1495.3	4600	3.5	010
Northwest-descending ridge	—	1.8	1497.1	4640	0.2	010
Switchback on a prominent ridge	—	1.8	1498.9	4330	-1.9	010
Fall Creek	w	1.3	1500.2	4050	-2.3	010
Cross a road and enter Castle Crags State Park	R	1.5	1501.7	3770	-2.0	011
Reach a closed road	R	3.2	1504.9	2420	-4.6	011
Paved Riverside Road	R	0.9	1505.8	2180	-2.9	011
General Delivery Castella, CA 96017 (530) 235-4413	PO,w,G,sh,r, R: 2.00m SW	0.0	1505.8	2180	-2.9	011
Interstate 5 near Castle Crags State Park, locked gate	—	0.7	1506.5	2130	-0.8	011
General Delivery Dunsmuir, CA 96025 (530) 235-0338	PO,w,G,M,L, R: 4.50m N	0.0	1506.5	2130	-0.8	P1
Junction with Kettlebelly Trail	—	0.5	1507.0	2420	6.3	P1
Root Creek trail	w: 0.25m N	1.3	1508.3	2590	1.4	P1
Leave Root Creek Trail	—	0.1	1508.4	2590	0.0	P1

NORTHERN CALIFORNIA

Landmark	Facilities	Diff	S->N	Elev	Gra	Map
Powerline saddle	—	0.1	1508.5	2650	6.5	P1
Bobs Hat Trail	—	0.5	1509.0	2820	3.7	P1
Winton Canyon Creek	w	1.0	1510.0	2875	0.6	P1
Sulphur Creek	w	3.1	1513.1	2750	-0.4	P2
Dog Trail	—	0.6	1513.7	3040	5.3	P2
North Fork tributary	w	1.8	1515.5	3110	0.4	P2
Section 31 tributary of North Fork Castle Creek, water upstream	w	1.0	1516.5	3370	2.8	P2
Forested saddle just beyond north boundary of Castle Crags State Park	—	3.6	1520.1	5620	6.8	P2
Cascading creek	w	0.4	1520.5	5750	3.5	P2
Densely vegetated creeklet	w	1.0	1521.5	5840	1.0	P2
West over to crest saddle 5983, water about 0.5m NW cross-country	w: 0.50m NW	0.7	1522.2	5983	2.2	P2
Ridge	—	2.0	1524.2	6320	1.8	P2
Soapstone Trail	—	0.5	1524.7	6500	3.9	P2
Peak 6835's south ridge	—	0.5	1525.2	6670	3.7	P2
Trinity Divide	w: 0.33m E	3.7	1528.9	6780	0.3	P4
Road 40N30	w,R: 0.33m E	2.3	1531.2	6460	-1.5	P4
Road 40N45	R	0.8	1532.0	6550	1.2	P4
Major saddle	—	2.1	1534.1	6770	1.1	P4
Spring	w	0.4	1534.5	6880	3.0	P4
East-dropping ridge with view of Lake Siskiyou	—	1.8	1536.3	7130	1.5	P5
Junction to beautiful Porcupine Lake	w: 0.25m W	0.5	1536.8	7220	2.0	P5
Climbs to a crest, junction to Toad Lake	—	0.3	1537.1	7300	2.9	P5
Trail 6W06	—	0.9	1538.0	7420	1.4	P5
Minor gap on the east ridge	—	0.9	1538.9	7620	2.4	P5

NORTHERN CALIFORNIA

Landmark	Facilities	Diff	S->N	Elev	Gra	Map
Trail intersection on a windy saddle	—	1.2	1540.1	7440	-1.6	P5
Spur trail to Deadfall Lake	w	2.1	1542.2	7250	-1.0	P5
Cross Deadfall Lakes Trail	—	0.3	1542.5	7230	-0.7	P5
Gully with a permanent spring	w	1.4	1543.9	7080	-1.2	P5
Parks Creek Road 42N17, shallow crest saddle	R	1.6	1545.5	6830	-1.7	P6
Cross an old trail by a small meadow's edge	—	3.0	1548.5	6770	-0.2	P6
Tops out on an adjacent ridge	—	1.6	1550.1	6650	-0.8	P6
Chilcoot Creek, spring-fed creeklet nearby	w	1.7	1551.8	6650	0.0	P6
Bull Lake crest saddle, meet old Sisson-Callahan Trail	—	2.1	1553.9	7100	2.3	P6
Secondary crest saddle	—	1.6	1555.5	6770	-2.2	P7
Two trail junctions, Little Trinity River Trail 7W01 and Sisson Trail	—	0.9	1556.4	6480	-3.5	P7
Next saddle after Peak 6857	—	1.3	1557.7	6160	-2.7	P7
Descend to another saddle	—	0.9	1558.6	6030	-1.6	P7
Meet 2 springs	w	1.3	1559.9	6080	0.4	P8
Cross a secondary ridge	—	1.1	1561.0	6100	0.2	P8
Masterson Meadow trail	w	0.7	1561.7	6110	0.2	P8
Grouse Creek Trail	—	0.2	1561.9	6130	1.1	P8
Masterson Meadow Lake seasonal creek	w	1.1	1563.0	6180	0.5	P8
Rocky knoll on a ridge	—	1.3	1564.3	6170	-0.1	P8
Trail switchbacks	—	1.3	1565.6	5790	-3.2	P8
Highway 3 at Scott Mountain Summit	w,R: 0.25m S	0.6	1566.2	5401	-7.1	P8
Enter Trinity Alps Wilderness	—	2.8	1569.0	6370	3.8	P9
Shallow crest gap	—	1.1	1570.1	6630	2.6	P9
Spring	w	0.8	1570.9	6440	-2.6	P9

NORTHERN CALIFORNIA

Landmark	Facilities	Diff	S->N	Elev	Gra	Map
Road 40N63	R	1.2	1572.1	6210	-2.1	P9
Mosquito Lake Creek	w	0.2	1572.3	6240	1.6	P9
Summer camp's primitive trail	—	0.5	1572.8	6460	4.8	P9
Junction to E. Boulder Lake/ Marshy Lakes	—	1.5	1574.3	7020	4.1	P1
Edge of talus slope	—	1.3	1575.6	7240	1.8	P9
East end of a windswept crest	—	0.9	1576.5	7400	1.9	P9
Another meadow, spring-fed creeklet	w	0.4	1576.9	7260	-3.8	P10
North end of a crest saddle, junction with Bloody Run Trail 8W04	—	0.9	1577.8	7160	-1.2	P10
On the crest with view of West Boulder Creek canyon	—	0.6	1578.4	7300	2.5	P10
Sage-covered crest saddle	—	0.4	1578.8	7190	-3.0	P10
Junction with Trail 8W05	—	1.2	1580.0	7170	-0.2	P10
Crest, junction with Trail 8W07 near Section Line Lake	—	0.3	1580.3	7230	2.2	P10
Swath of alders	w	1.4	1581.7	6850	-2.9	P10
Crest saddle with trail 9W01	—	1.2	1582.9	6780	-0.6	P11
Saddle's west end, another branch of Trail 9W01	—	0.1	1583.0	6780	0.0	P11
Narrow crest	—	0.5	1583.5	6660	-2.6	P11
South Fork Lakes Trail 9W13	—	1.5	1585.0	5810	-6.2	P11
South Fork Scott River	w	0.2	1585.2	5780	-1.6	P11
Alder-lined creeklet	w	0.5	1585.7	5880	2.2	P11
Forest Highway 93 at Carter Meadows Summit	R	0.4	1586.1	6160	7.6	P11
Crest saddle with views of South Fork Lakes canyon	—	1.1	1587.2	6660	4.9	P11
Under a crest saddle	—	1.7	1588.9	6910	1.6	P11
Climb to a jeep trail	—	2.3	1591.2	6940	0.1	P13
Jeep trail to Siphon Lake	w: 0.75m W	0.2	1591.4	7030	4.9	P13

NORTHERN CALIFORNIA

Landmark	Facilities	Diff	S->N	Elev	Gra	Map
Bingham Lake's outlet creek under boulders	—	1.8	1593.2	6940	-0.5	P13
Alder-choked creek	w	2.3	1595.5	6700	-1.1	P13
Blakes Fork creek under boulders	—	0.5	1596.0	6700	0.0	P13
Curve northeast, 250 feet below Statue Lake, water from creek	w	1.1	1597.1	6930	2.3	P13
Trail 9W09	—	1.1	1598.2	6710	-2.2	P14
Paynes Lake Creek	w	2.2	1600.4	6460	-1.2	P14
Glacial bowl	w	0.7	1601.1	6620	2.5	P14
Junction to Taylor Lake	—	1.5	1602.6	6970	2.5	P14
Jeep-road junction to Upper Ruffey Lake	R	2.0	1604.6	6910	-0.3	P14
Somes Bar-Etna Road at Etna Summit	R	1.7	1606.3	5960	-6.1	P14
General Delivery Etna, CA 96027 (530) 467-3981	PO,w,G,M,L,sh, R: 10.40m NE	0.0	1606.3	5960	-6.1	P14
Southeast end of Razor Ridge	—	3.7	1610.0	6690	2.1	Q1
Cross a more persistent creeklet	w	1.0	1611.0	6450	-2.6	Q1
Reach another creek	w	2.0	1613.0	6170	-1.5	Q2
Headwaters of Babs Fork Kiddler Creek	—	0.9	1613.9	6290	1.4	Q2
Saddle just north of Peak 6667	—	1.4	1615.3	6430	1.1	Q2
Shelly Lake's outlet creek	w	1.7	1617.0	6150	-1.8	Q2
Junction with Shelly Meadows Trail	—	0.3	1617.3	6220	2.5	Q2
Shelly Fork Trail/Shelly Meadows Trail	—	0.2	1617.5	6340	6.5	Q2
Saddle below Peak 7109	—	2.2	1619.7	6410	0.3	Q3
Creeklet with campsites	w	0.3	1620.0	6190	-8.0	Q3
Fisher Lake	w	0.4	1620.4	6220	0.8	Q3
Marten Lake	w	0.3	1620.7	6360	5.1	Q3

NORTHERN CALIFORNIA

Landmark	Facilities	Diff	S->N	Elev	Gra	Map
Junction to older PCT route to Kidder Lake Trail	—	1.2	1621.9	6560	1.8	Q3
Conspicuous saddle	—	0.5	1622.4	6870	6.7	Q3
Junction with older PCT segment	—	1.1	1623.5	7180	3.1	Q3
Saddle, meet Shackleford Creek Trail	—	1.7	1625.2	6590	-3.8	Q4
Junction to Red Rock Valley Trail/ Cold Springs	w: 0.25m S	1.6	1626.8	6310	-1.9	Q5
Second set of trails to Red Rock Valley Trail/west Cold Spring Trail	w: 0.30m S	0.3	1627.1	6370	2.2	Q5
Shadow Lake Trail	—	0.3	1627.4	6480	4.0	Q5
Soft Water Spring	w	0.6	1628.0	6580	1.8	Q5
Junction to Sky High Valley trail	—	0.9	1628.9	6400	-2.2	Q5
Junction to Big Elk Lake	—	0.5	1629.4	6232	-3.6	Q5
Marble Valley Guard Station/ Canyon Creek Trail	w	1.0	1630.4	5700	-5.8	Q5
Marble Gap Trail, water nearby	w	0.3	1630.7	5840	5.1	Q5
Junction to Big Rock Camp	—	2.2	1632.9	6640	3.9	Q5
Jumpoff, a low point on a narrow crest	—	0.4	1633.3	6650	0.3	Q5
Notch in southwest end of Cayenne Ridge	—	2.2	1635.5	6190	-2.3	Q6
Paradise Lake	w	0.2	1635.7	6130	-3.3	Q6
Junction to Bear Lake/Turk Lake	—	1.6	1637.3	6580	3.1	Q6
Big Ridge Cutoff Trail, views	—	0.7	1638.0	6800	3.4	Q6
Buckhorn Spring	w	3.3	1641.3	6570	-0.8	Q6
Small flat with tiny pond	w	0.3	1641.6	6300	-9.8	Q7
Huckleberry Mountain Trail	—	1.0	1642.6	6020	-3.0	Q7
Cross a good road	R	1.5	1644.1	5300	-5.2	Q7
Cross another good road	R	1.0	1645.1	4800	-5.4	Q7
Last logging road crossing	R	0.9	1646.0	4370	-5.2	Q7

NORTHERN CALIFORNIA

Landmark	Facilities	Diff	S->N	Elev	Gra	Map
Grider Creek Trail at Road 46N72/ Cold Spring Creek	w,R	2.0	1648.0	3200	-6.4	Q7
Footbridge across Grider Creek	w	0.8	1648.8	2870	-4.5	Q7
Second footbridge across Grider Creek	w	1.3	1650.1	2640	-1.9	Q7
Third footbridge across Grider Creek	w	1.7	1651.8	2330	-2.0	Q8
Bark Shanty Creek	w	0.4	1652.2	2280	-1.4	Q8
Junction with Old Grider Creek Trail	w	1.8	1654.0	1920	-2.2	Q8
Grider Creek Trail at Grider Creek Campground	w	1.6	1655.6	1700	-1.5	Q8
Road 46N66	R	0.3	1655.9	1680	-0.7	Q8
Last bridge across Grider Creek	w	0.8	1656.7	1520	-2.2	Q8
Junction with a spur road	R	1.5	1658.2	1400	-0.9	Q9
Highway 96	R	2.4	1660.6	1435	0.2	Q9
Klamath River	—	0.5	1661.1	1430	-0.1	Q9
Highway 96 at Seiad Valley	R	1.0	1662.1	1371	-0.6	Q9
General Delivery Seiad Valley, CA 96086 (530) 496-3211	PO,w,G,M,r,R	0.0	1662.1	1371	-0.6	Q9
School House Gulch	—	0.5	1662.6	1380	0.2	R1
Lower Devils Peak Lookout Trail 12W04	—	0.3	1662.9	1380	0.0	R1
Junction to a trail paralleling Highway 96	R	0.2	1663.1	1600	12.0	R1
Fern Spring	w	0.7	1663.8	1900	4.7	R1
Lookout Spring	w	4.6	1668.4	4800	6.9	R1
Lower Devils Peak saddle	—	0.2	1668.6	5020	12.0	R1
Darkey Creek Trail	—	0.6	1669.2	5170	2.7	R1
Upper Devils Peak's western arm	—	1.0	1670.2	5820	7.1	R1
Portuguese Creek Trail 12W03	—	1.2	1671.4	5760	-0.5	R1

NORTHERN CALIFORNIA

Landmark	Facilities	Diff	S->N	Elev	Gra	Map
Boundary Trail 12W47	—	0.3	1671.7	5940	6.5	R1
Spring in spongy ground	w	0.8	1672.5	5760	-2.4	R1
Kangaroo Mountain's east ridge	—	0.5	1673.0	5900	3.0	R1
Spur trail to a jeep road	R	0.2	1673.2	5900	0.0	R1
Cross the jeep road	R	1.0	1674.2	5710	-2.1	R1
Junction with Horse Camp Trail 958 to Echo Lake	—	0.5	1674.7	5900	4.1	R1
Cook and Green Pass	w: 0.10m NW	2.5	1677.2	4770	-4.9	R2
Trail 11W02	—	2.8	1680.0	6080	5.1	R2
Horse Creek Trail 11W01	—	2.2	1682.2	6040	-0.2	R2
Junction to Lowdens Cabin site	w: 0.12m SE	0.3	1682.5	6040	0.0	R3
Junction with the old PCT	w: 0.10m SW	2.0	1684.5	5950	-0.5	R3
Road 47N81	R	2.4	1686.9	6310	1.6	R3
Junction to Buckhorn Camp, Alex Hole Camp entrance	w: 0.30m S	3.1	1690.0	6630	1.1	R4
Mud Springs spur road	w,R: 0.20m NW	2.3	1692.3	6730	0.5	R5
Road 40S01	R	1.6	1693.9	6250	-3.3	R5
Road north of Bearground Spring	w,R	0.8	1694.7	5930	-4.3	R5
Wards Fork Gap	—	1.3	1696.0	5317	-5.1	R5
Bridge over Donomore Creek	w	1.5	1697.5	5600	2.0	R5

Northern California

OREGON

WASHINGTON

Cascade Range

Mt Adams
Trout Lake

Bingen-White
Salmon

Cascade Locks
(Bridge of the Gods) · mi 2153.5 · Vancouver WA · Cascade Locks

141

Hood River

The Dalles

Portland

14

84

Eagle Creek

Mt Hood

G 51.7 miles

26

Timberline

35

Timberline Lodge · mi 2107.3

Government Camp

Barlow Pass · mi 2102.4

Salem

5

Cascade

Olalie Butte

Olalie Lake · mi 2053.1

Olalie

F 112.9 miles

OREGON

Albany

Detroit

Mt Jefferson

Santiam Pass

Three Fingered Jack

Hwy 20 (Santiam Pass - Sisters & Bend) · mi 2006.9

20

Mt Washington

Sisters

Hwy 242 · mi 1989.5
(Mackenzie Pass - Sisters & Bend)

126

McKenzie Pass

North Sister

20

Eugene

Middle Sister

Bend

58

E 75.7 miles

Willamette Pass

South Sister

97

Elk Lake Trail Junction (Elk Lake Resort) · mi 1958.3

Hwy 58 (Willamette Pass) · mi 1913.8

(no Amtrak)

Shelter Cove Resort · mi 1912.2

Shelter Cove

Crescent Lake Campground (on OST) · mi

Diamond Peak
Crescent Lake Campground

Crescent Lake
(no Amtrak)

D 61.3 miles

Windigo Pass (Oregon Skyline Trail Jct.) · mi 1882.9

Mt Theilson

Chemult

Hwy 138 (Cascade Crest) · mi 1852.5

138

Crater Lake - North Rim · mi 1841

230

Crater Lake - South Rim (Rim Village) · mi 1834.9

Crater Lake

Hwy 62 (Mazama Village) · mi 1830.4

Mazama Village

C 72.1 miles

Grant Pass

62

Sky Lakes Trail Junction (PCT Alt) · mi 1798.2

Mt McLaughlin

Sky Lakes

97

Hwy 140 (Fish Lake) · mi 1780.4

Medford

140

Klamath Falls

B 53.8 miles

Ashland

Interstate 5 (Calahan's-Ashland) · mi 1726.6

Callahan's

66

California / Oregon Border · mi 1698.8

OREGON
CALIFORNIA

A R 64.5 miles

5

Pacific Crest Trail

Seiad Valley · mi 1662.1 · Seiad Valley

96

Pacific Crest Trail
Oregon
OR Border - WA Border
Cartography by: Magellan (2013)
(Andrew Alfred-Duggan, Toronto-Canada)
www.andrewmaps.com

Weed

Oregon

OREGON

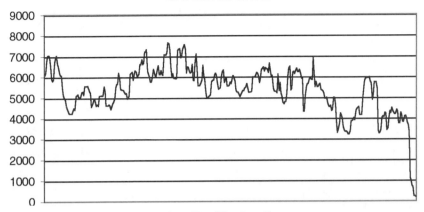

**Elevation Profile for Oregon
From California-Oregon Border**

Section Total Mileage: 456.0 miles

Landmark	Facilities	Diff	S->N	Elev	Gra	Map
California-Oregon Border	—	1.3	1698.8	6080	4.0	R6
Logging road saddle, cross Road 2025	R	0.1	1698.9	6210	14.3	R6
West ridge of twin topped Observation Peak	—	1.6	1700.5	6750	3.7	R6
Observation Gap	—	1.2	1701.7	7030	2.5	R6
Just below Jackson Gap	—	1.2	1702.9	7040	0.1	R6
Spur road to Sheep Camp Spring	w,R	0.3	1703.2	6920	-4.3	R6
Wrangle Gap	—	2.3	1705.5	6496	-2.0	R7
Siskiyou Gap	—	3.8	1709.3	5890	-1.7	R8
Cross Road 40S12	R	0.3	1709.6	5800	-3.3	R8
5-way road junction on Long John Saddle	w,R: 0.50m W	1.3	1710.9	5880	0.7	R8
Open crest saddle	—	2.1	1713.0	6710	4.3	R8
Cross a spur road	R	0.8	1713.8	6900	2.6	R8

OREGON

Landmark	Facilities	Diff	S->N	Elev	Gra	Map
Another saddle	—	1.1	1714.9	7030	1.3	R9
Grouse Gap, Road 40S30	w,R: 0.20m S	1.0	1715.9	6630	-4.3	R9
Cross Road 40S15 to Mt. Ashland Campground	w,R: 0.50m NE	1.9	1717.8	6480	-0.9	R9
Cross Road 20	R	1.5	1719.3	6160	-2.3	R9
Road 2080	R	0.4	1719.7	6060	-2.7	R9
General Delivery Ashland, OR 97520 (541) 552-1622	PO,w,G,M,L,R: 12.40m N	0.0	1719.7	6060	-2.7	R9
Saddle below the Ashland Inn, water at the Inn	w	1.5	1721.2	5490	-4.1	R10
Another saddle	—	0.8	1722.0	5110	-5.2	R10
Another saddle with 4 roads	R	0.8	1722.8	4990	-1.6	R10
Spring-fed gully	w	2.1	1724.9	4880	-0.6	R10
Road past a spring-fed gully	R	0.4	1725.3	4610	-7.3	R10
Cross another road	R	0.1	1725.4	4470	-15.0	R10
Cross a third road	R	0.1	1725.5	4360	-12.0	R10
Path ends at abandoned segment of old Highway 99	R	0.8	1726.3	4250	-1.5	R10
Highway 99, just below Interstate 5 near Mt. Ashland Road 20	R	0.3	1726.6	4240	-0.4	R10
Callahan's Restaurant and Country Store, 0.9m N	w,G,M: 0.90m N	0.0	1726.6	4240	-0.4	R10
General Delivery Ashland, OR 97520 (541) 552-1622	PO,w,G,M,L, R: 12.90m N	0.0	1726.6	4240	-0.4	R10
Resumption of PCT after I-5	—	0.5	1727.1	4380	3.0	B1
Reach a spring	w	0.9	1728.0	4490	1.3	B1
Major intersection	—	1.3	1729.3	4420	-0.6	B1
Atop a broad saddle	—	1.7	1731.0	5080	4.2	B1
Cross upper Pilot Rock Jeep Road	R	0.2	1731.2	5120	2.2	B1
Reach the first gate	—	0.9	1732.1	5160	0.5	B1

Oregon

OREGON

Landmark	Facilities	Diff	S->N	Elev	Gra	Map
Crest saddle	—	0.7	1732.8	4990	-2.6	B1
North to a crest	—	1.2	1734.0	5020	0.3	B2
Trail's resumption on our left	—	0.2	1734.2	5040	1.1	B2
Cross the jeep road a second time	R	0.8	1735.0	5270	3.1	B2
Very refreshing fenced-in spring	w	1.2	1736.2	5290	0.2	B2
Descend northeast to a saddle	—	0.3	1736.5	5140	-5.4	B2
South slope of Little Pilot Peak	—	0.9	1737.4	5550	4.9	B2
Dips to north side of a saddle	—	0.1	1737.5	5550	0.0	B2
Spring-fed tub, 80 yards northwest down from the trail	w	0.8	1738.3	5550	0.0	B2
Meet an old trail	—	0.2	1738.5	5560	0.5	B2
Shaded saddle	—	0.6	1739.1	5420	-2.5	B2
Soda Springs Road	R	0.5	1739.6	5300	-2.6	B3
Hobart Bluff spur trail	—	0.9	1740.5	5220	-1.0	B3
Highway 66 at Green Springs Summit	w,R: 0.25m NE	3.4	1743.9	4551	-2.1	B3
Road 100-90	R	1.4	1745.3	4700	1.2	B5
Greensprings Mountain Road	R	0.5	1745.8	4840	3.0	B5
Cross a spur road	R	0.7	1746.5	4940	1.6	B4
Water faucet (may be gone), fed by an uphill spring	w	0.6	1747.1	4800	-2.5	B4
Ashland lateral canal, dry gully	—	0.5	1747.6	4600	-4.3	B4
Second gully meets a trail to Little Hyatt Reservoir	w: 0.25m N	0.9	1748.5	4670	0.8	B5
Hyatt Lake Recreation Road 100-90	R	0.2	1748.7	4610	-3.3	B5
Hyatt Lake Campground spur trail, past old roads to a road fork	R	1.5	1750.2	5090	3.5	B5

Oregon

OREGON

Landmark	Facilities	Diff	S->N	Elev	Gra	Map
Hyatt Lake Resort Attn: (Your Name) PCT Hiker 7900 Hyatt Prairie Road Ashland, OR 97520 (541) 482-3331 Via UPS only!	w,G,M,sh,r, R: 0.75m N	0.0	1750.2	5090	3.5	B5
Road 39-3E-15	R	2.1	1752.3	5100	0.1	B5
Wildcat Glades Road 39-3E-11	R	0.9	1753.2	5090	-0.1	B5
Cross an older road to Wildcat Glades and reach a seeping creek	R	0.2	1753.4	5100	0.5	B5
Reaches the main summit	—	1.0	1754.4	5540	4.8	B5
Almost touch a saddle	—	0.5	1754.9	5310	-5.0	B6
Cross a road that climbs southwest to a rock quarry	R	2.0	1756.9	4620	-3.7	B6
Junction to Soda Creek	w: 0.50m S	0.1	1757.0	4620	0.0	B6
Secondary road climbs east	R	0.2	1757.2	4620	0.0	B6
Cross a little-used road to Klum Landing Campground	w,R: 0.30m E	0.9	1758.1	4670	0.6	B6
Drops northeast to a well-maintained road	R	0.2	1758.3	4610	-3.3	B6
Grizzly Creek	w	0.5	1758.8	4440	-3.7	B6
Moon Prairie Road	R	0.4	1759.2	4580	3.8	B6
Keno Access Road	R	0.8	1760.0	4720	1.9	B6
Old road before the newer logging road	R	0.2	1760.2	4790	3.8	B6
Brush Mountain Road	R	0.6	1760.8	4960	3.1	B7
Old logging road	R	1.5	1762.3	5480	3.8	B7
Approach Griffin Pass Road 2520	R	0.5	1762.8	5640	3.5	B7
Parallel Road 2520 to a crossing, east to Big Springs creeklet	w,R: 0.10m E	0.2	1763.0	5670	1.6	B7
Rogue River National Forest boundary	—	1.7	1764.7	6190	3.3	B7
Faint spur trail to Road 650	R	1.0	1765.7	5880	-3.4	B8

Oregon

OREGON

Landmark	Facilities	Diff	S->N	Elev	Gra	Map
Cross a closed road	R	1.2	1766.9	5390	-4.4	B8
Cross Road 3802	R	0.3	1767.2	5390	0.0	B8
Dead Indian Road	R	1.9	1769.1	5360	-0.2	B8
Junction to Brown Mountain Shelter	w: 0.10m W	1.7	1770.8	5330	-0.2	B8
Cross Road 3720-740	R	0.2	1771.0	5270	-3.3	B8
South Fork Little Butte Creek	—	2.2	1773.2	5180	-0.4	B9
Minor ridge	—	1.4	1774.6	5210	0.2	B9
Fish Lake Trail 1014	w: 0.33m W	5.8	1780.4	4940	-0.5	B9
Highway 140 near Fish Lake	R	0.2	1780.6	4980	2.2	B9
Junction to large trailhead parking lot	w	0.3	1780.9	5100	4.3	C1
Mt. McLoughlin Trail 3716	—	4.0	1784.9	6110	2.7	C1
Freye Lake spur trail	w: 0.25m N	0.2	1785.1	6190	4.3	C1
Leave Mt. McLoughlin Trail, westbound	—	0.2	1785.3	6240	2.7	C1
Twin Ponds Trail to Summit Lake	w: 0.40m NW	3.7	1789.0	5840	-1.2	C3
Cat Hill Way Trail 992	—	1.6	1790.6	6100	1.8	C3
Broad saddle	—	1.6	1792.2	6300	1.4	C4
Another saddle, junction to Christi's Spring	w: 0.03m N	1.2	1793.4	6240	-0.5	C4
Red Lake Trail 987	—	1.1	1794.5	6020	-2.2	C4
Northern end of Red Lake Trail	—	2.7	1797.2	6070	0.2	C5
Sky Lakes Trail 3762	—	1.0	1798.2	6140	0.8	C5
Spur trail to overlook	—	2.5	1800.7	6600	2.0	C5
Wickiup Trail 986/3728	—	1.0	1801.7	6585	-0.2	C5
Divide Trail 3717	—	1.2	1802.9	6840	2.3	C5
Hemlock Lake Trail 985	—	1.0	1803.9	6600	-2.6	C5
Snow Lakes Trail 3739	w: 0.20m NE	0.2	1804.1	6670	3.8	C6
Devils Peak Trail 984	—	1.7	1805.8	7210	3.4	C6

Oregon

OREGON

Landmark	Facilities	Diff	S->N	Elev	Gra	Map
Abandoned segment of Devils Peak Trail	—	0.2	1806.0	7190	-1.1	C6
Devils Peak/Lee Peak saddle	—	0.5	1806.5	7320	2.8	C6
Junction to Seven Lakes Trail 981	—	2.4	1808.9	6250	-4.8	C6
Sevenmile Trail 3703	—	0.7	1809.6	6130	-1.9	C6
Honeymoon Creek	w	0.5	1810.1	5980	-3.3	C6
Leave Sevenmile Trail	—	2.1	1812.2	5760	-1.1	C7
Meet Middle Fork Basin Trail to Ranger Springs	w: 0.90m SW	0.2	1812.4	5750	-0.5	C7
Junction with Big Bunchgrass Trail 1089A	—	1.0	1813.4	6020	2.9	C7
McKie Camp Trail 1089	—	0.9	1814.3	6380	4.3	C7
Jack Spring spur trail	w: 0.50m NW	2.7	1817.0	6190	-0.8	C7
Water Alert (↓): 15.5m						
Abandoned Dry Creek Trail 3701	—	2.4	1819.4	6040	-0.7	C8
South end of Stuart Falls Trail 1078	—	0.2	1819.6	6050	0.5	C8
Second old, closed road	R	5.6	1825.2	6290	0.5	C8
Top of narrow, open flat	—	2.4	1827.6	6550	1.2	C8
Highway 62, close to Mazama Campground	w,G,sh,R: 1.30m E	2.8	1830.4	6108	-1.7	C9
General Delivery Crater Lake, OR 97604 (541) 594-3115	PO,w,G,M,L,r, R: 4.50m NE	0.0	1830.4	6108	-1.7	C10
Second fault-line gully	—	0.8	1831.2	6310	2.7	C9
Descend to a closed road	R	0.6	1831.8	6130	-3.3	C9
Dutton Creek	w	0.7	1832.5	6080	-0.8	C9
Water Alert (↓): 28.3m						
Water Alert (↑): 16.0m						
Crater Lake Rim Village Junction	—	2.4	1834.9	7075	4.5	C10

Oregon

OREGON

Landmark	Facilities	Diff	S->N	Elev	Gra	Map
Crater Lake Lodge Attn: (Your Name) PCT Hiker 565 Rim Drive Crater Lake, OR 97604 (541) 594-2255 x3200 Via UPS Only!	w,G,M,L, R: 2.80m SE	0.0	1834.9	7075	4.5	C10
General Delivery Crater Lake, OR 97604 (541) 594-3115	PO,w,G,M,L,r, R: 2.80m SE	0.0	1834.9	7075	4.5	C10
Discovery Point	—	1.5	1836.4	7050	-0.2	C9
Junction to Lightning Spring	w: 0.75m W	0.8	1837.2	7172	1.7	C9
Wizard Island Overlook	—	1.4	1838.6	7600	3.3	C11
Cross Rim Drive	R	2.4	1841.0	7260	-1.5	C12
Junction with PCT equestrian route	—	2.7	1843.7	6510	-3.0	C12
Walk east to a road fork, and branch northeast	R	2.9	1846.6	5985	-2.0	C13
Back on trail tread	—	1.3	1847.9	6150	1.4	C13
North boundary of Crater Lake National Park	—	2.7	1850.6	5942	-0.8	C13
Highway 138 near the Cascade crest	R	1.9	1852.5	5920	-0.1	C13
South end of North Crater Trail 1410	—	0.1	1852.6	5910	-1.1	D1
Old, abandoned Summit Rock Road	R	0.5	1853.1	5935	0.5	D1
Mt. Thielsen Trail	—	5.3	1858.4	7260	2.7	D3
New Mt. Thielsen Trail 1456	—	0.3	1858.7	7330	2.5	D3
Head to northwest ridge	—	1.0	1859.7	7370	0.4	D3
Thielsen Creek	w	1.1	1860.8	6930	-4.3	D3
Water Alert (↓): 16.5m						
Water Alert (↑): 28.3m						
Thielsen Creek Trail 1449	—	0.1	1860.9	6960	3.3	D3
Junction with Howlock Mountain Trail 1448	—	3.1	1864.0	7320	1.3	D3

Oregon

OREGON

Landmark	Facilities	Diff	S->N	Elev	Gra	Map
Climb to a crest saddle	—	0.4	1864.4	7435	3.1	D4
Highest point in Oregon-Washington PCT segment	—	1.3	1865.7	7560	1.0	D4
Northeast of saddle past Tipsoo Peak	—	0.8	1866.5	7300	-3.5	D4
Maidu Lake Trail 3725A	w: 0.90m NW	4.3	1870.8	6190	-2.8	D5
Crossing of county-line ridge	—	1.3	1872.1	6490	2.5	D7
Descend to a crest saddle	—	2.3	1874.4	6470	-0.1	D7
Diagonal northeast to a saddle	—	1.9	1876.3	6300	-1.0	D6
Tolo Camp, junction to Six Horse Spring	w: 0.33m E	0.7	1877.0	6190	-1.7	D6
Water Alert (↑): 16.2m						
Traverse over to another saddle	—	0.6	1877.6	6325	2.4	D6
Tenas Trail 1445	—	1.3	1878.9	6610	2.4	D8
Spur trail to parking area by old Cascade Lakes Road	R	3.7	1882.6	5845	-2.2	D8
Windigo Pass, new Cascade Lakes Road 60, water cross country 0.1m E	w,R: 0.10m E	0.3	1882.9	5820	-0.9	D8
Minor crest saddle to lakelet	w: 0.10m NW	2.3	1885.2	6620	3.8	D8
Saddle by southwest ridge of Cowhorn Mountain	—	1.6	1886.8	7100	3.3	D8
Stagnant pool	w	3.1	1889.9	6380	-2.5	D9
Summit Lake's south shore	w	4.1	1894.0	5560	-2.2	D9
Road 700	R	0.2	1894.2	5570	0.5	D9
Road 6010 near Summit Lake Campground	R	1.4	1895.6	5590	0.2	D9
Leaving west shore of last unmapped lake	w	1.1	1896.7	5670	0.8	D9
South shore of one accessible lake	w	0.9	1897.6	5860	2.3	D9
Northwest up a switchback, plenty of ponds north on PCT	—	2.8	1900.4	6560	2.7	D11

Oregon

OREGON

Landmark	Facilities	Diff	S->N	Elev	Gra	Map
North shore of a green, unnamed lake, plenty of ponds south on PCT	w	7.2	1907.6	6030	-0.8	D11
Descend to an even larger lake	w	0.6	1908.2	5840	-3.4	D11
Junction to well-hidden Midnight Lake	w: 0.05m E	2.5	1910.7	5370	-2.0	D13
Pengra Pass	—	1.5	1912.2	5003	-2.7	D13
Shelter Cove Resort Attn: (Your Name) PCT Hiker West Odell Lake Road, Highway 58 Crescent Lake, OR 97425 (541) 433-2548 Held for 2 weeks Via UPS Only!	PO,w,G,sh,r,R: 1.40m SE	0.0	1912.2	5003	-2.7	D13
Old Oregon Skyline Trail	—	0.5	1912.7	5040	0.8	D13
Highway 58 near Willamette Pass	R	1.1	1913.8	5090	0.5	D13
Trailhead-parking spur trail	—	0.2	1914.0	5130	2.2	E1
Ridge above South (Lower) Rosary Lake	w	2.0	1916.0	5730	3.3	E1
Middle Rosary Lake	w	0.6	1916.6	5830	1.8	E1
North Rosary Lake	w	0.3	1916.9	5830	0.0	E1
Maiden Lake Trail 41	—	0.6	1917.5	6060	4.2	E1
Switchback west to a saddle	—	0.5	1918.0	6170	2.4	E1
Minor saddle	—	1.3	1919.3	6070	-0.8	E2
Maiden Peak Trail	—	1.1	1920.4	5800	-2.7	E2
Bobby Lake Trail 3663	—	2.2	1922.6	5440	-1.8	E2
Moore Creek Trail 40 to Bobby Lake	w: 0.25m E	0.2	1922.8	5470	1.6	E2
Climb northwest to a saddle	—	1.4	1924.2	5980	4.0	E2
Twin Peaks Trail 3595	—	1.3	1925.5	6220	2.0	E3
Cluster of 3 ponds	—	2.4	1927.9	6320	0.5	E3
Charlton Lake Trail 3570	w: 0.10m SE	2.5	1930.4	5725	-2.6	E3
Road 5897	R	0.6	1931.0	5840	2.1	E3
Lily Lake Trail 19	w: 0.75m NE	1.4	1932.4	5965	1.0	E3

OREGON

Landmark	Facilities	Diff	S->N	Elev	Gra	Map
Taylor Lake	w	3.3	1935.7	5550	-1.4	E5
Road 600 at Irish Lake	w,R	0.3	1936.0	5549	0.0	E5
Riffle Lake	w	0.8	1936.8	5575	0.4	E5
Climb to a higher ridge	—	1.2	1938.0	5730	1.4	E5
East shore of Brahma Lake	w	0.6	1938.6	5657	-1.3	E5
Jezebel Lake	w	1.1	1939.7	5855	2.0	E5
Stormy Lake	w	1.0	1940.7	6045	2.1	E5
Blaze Lake	w	0.3	1941.0	5950	-3.4	E5
Cougar Flat	—	2.1	1943.1	5750	-1.0	E6
Tadpole Lake	w	2.0	1945.1	5340	-2.2	E6
Elk Creek and Winopee Lake trails	—	0.4	1945.5	5250	-2.4	E6
Snowshoe Lake Trail 33	w	1.2	1946.7	5250	0.0	E6
Mink Lake Loop Trail 3526	w	0.4	1947.1	5160	-2.4	E6
Spur trail to Moody Lake	w: 0.10m N	1.5	1948.6	5040	-0.9	E6
Cliff Lake Trail, Mink Lake Loop Trail 3526	w	0.8	1949.4	5130	1.2	E6
Climb gently to a seasonal creek	—	0.8	1950.2	5225	1.3	E6
Goose Rock and Senoj Lake trails	—	0.6	1950.8	5330	1.9	E6
Large, east-end campsite	w	0.4	1951.2	5320	-0.3	E6
Island Lake	w	0.5	1951.7	5438	2.6	E6
Dumbbell Lake	w	0.7	1952.4	5502	1.0	E6
Past many ponds to a low divide	—	2.2	1954.6	5660	0.8	E6
Junction with old OST	—	0.5	1955.1	5460	-4.3	E7
Sunset Lake Trail 3517A	—	1.9	1957.0	5235	-1.3	E7
Island Meadow Trail to Elk Lake 3/3517	—	1.3	1958.3	5250	0.1	E7

OREGON

Landmark	Facilities	Diff	S->N	Elev	Gra	Map
Elk Lake Resort Attn: (Your Name) PCT Hiker 60000 Century Drive Bend, OR 97701 (541) 480-7378 Via UPS or FedEx Only! $5 handling fee	w,G,M,L,sh, R: 1.10m E	0.0	1958.3	5250	0.1	E7
Horse Lake Trail 2/3516	—	1.3	1959.6	5300	0.4	E7
Camelot Lake	w	4.6	1964.2	5980	1.6	E9
Sisters Mirror Lake	w	0.1	1964.3	5980	0.0	E9
Junction with Nash Lake Trail 3527 and Mirror Lake Trail 20	—	0.4	1964.7	5990	0.3	E9
Junction with Wickiup Plain Trail	—	0.3	1965.0	6030	1.4	E9
Broad county-line divide	—	1.2	1966.2	6210	1.6	E9
Side trail to Wickiup Plain Trail	—	0.5	1966.7	6160	-1.1	E9
Descend to a creek	w	1.2	1967.9	6010	-1.4	E10
North Fork of Mesa Creek	w	0.8	1968.7	5700	-4.2	E10
Junction with James Creek Trail	—	0.6	1969.3	5920	4.0	E10
Cross Hinton Creek	w	2.1	1971.4	6320	2.1	E10
Cross Separation Creek	w	0.5	1971.9	6400	1.7	E10
Clear lakelet with good campsites	w	0.4	1972.3	6460	1.6	E10
Foley Ridge Trail 3511	—	1.3	1973.6	6270	-1.6	E10
Linton Meadows Trail	—	1.7	1975.3	6440	1.1	E10
Obsidian Trail 3528	w	2.1	1977.4	6380	-0.3	E12
Glacier Way Trail 3528A	w	1.6	1979.0	6370	-0.1	E12
White Branch Creek	—	0.9	1979.9	6210	-1.9	E12
Minnie Scott Spring	w	2.2	1982.1	6650	2.2	E12
Scott Trail 3551	—	0.9	1983.0	6300	-4.2	E12
South Matthieu Lake	w	2.5	1985.5	6040	-1.1	E12
South junction with old OST route to North Matthieu Lake	—	0.1	1985.6	6070	3.3	E12

OREGON

Landmark	Facilities	Diff	S->N	Elev	Gra	Map
North junction with old OST route to North Matthieu Lake	—	2.1	1987.7	5450	-3.2	E13
Trail to Lava Camp Lake, junction to a large trailhead parking area	w: 0.25m NE	0.7	1988.4	5310	-2.2	E13
Water Alert (↓): 16.5m						
McKenzie Highway (242)	R	1.1	1989.5	5280	-0.3	E13
Town of Sisters	w,G: 15.00m NE	0.0	1989.5	5280	-0.3	E13
Highway 242 at McKenzie Pass, small trailhead parking area	R	0.3	1989.8	5210	-2.5	E13
Spur trail to summit of Little Belknap	—	2.3	1992.1	6120	4.3	F1
Fresh-looking lava flow	—	2.5	1994.6	5320	-3.5	F1
Washington Ponds spur trail, very difficult to find	—	2.5	1997.1	5710	1.7	F1
Coldwater Spring	—	2.4	1999.5	5200	-2.3	F1
Unmarked climber's trail to Washington Peak	—	0.5	2000.0	5050	-3.3	F2
Descend north to fork with broad trail	—	0.9	2000.9	4760	-3.5	F2
Old Santiam Wagon Road	R	2.0	2002.9	4680	-0.4	F2
Lily-pad pond	w	2.0	2004.9	4790	0.6	F2
Water Alert (↑): 16.8m						
Cross Santiam Highway (US Highway 20), junction to Douthit Spring	w,R: 0.30m E	2.0	2006.9	4810	0.1	F3
Santiam Lake Trail 3491	—	1.4	2008.3	5200	3.0	F3
Curve north-northwest, cross-country hike to Summit Lake	w: 0.40m NE	2.5	2010.8	6000	3.5	F3
Round the peak's northwest spur	—	2.6	2013.4	6390	1.6	F3
Saddle along the Cascade divide	—	0.5	2013.9	6500	2.4	F3
Minto Pass Trail 3437 south to Wasco Lake	w: 0.25m S	3.2	2017.1	5350	-3.9	F4
Wasco Lake loop trail (#65)	w: 0.50m SE	0.5	2017.6	5430	1.7	F4

OREGON

Landmark	Facilities	Diff	S->N	Elev	Gra	Map
Southeast spur of Peak 6488	—	2.2	2019.8	6210	3.9	F4
Rockpile Lake	w	1.0	2020.8	6250	0.4	F4
Trail forks as Trail 69	—	0.5	2021.3	6140	-2.4	F4
Swallow Lake Trail 3488	—	1.0	2022.3	6300	1.7	F4
Reach a saddle	—	1.2	2023.5	6400	0.9	F5
Unsigned trail to emerald Carl Lake	w: 1.00m SE	0.9	2024.4	6240	-1.9	F5
Small, grassy meadow, water in pond	w	1.7	2026.1	6240	0.0	F5
Escarpment where Mt. Jefferson towers above	—	0.4	2026.5	6340	2.7	F5
Unsigned trail climbs back to divide	—	0.7	2027.2	6130	-3.3	F5
Start of Pamelia Lake alternate route, reach a saddle	—	0.5	2027.7	5910	-4.8	F5
West shore of placid Shale Lake	w	1.8	2029.5	5910	0.0	F5
End of Pamelia Lake alternate route, junction with old OST	—	4.5	2034.0	4320	-3.8	F5
Cross Milk Creek	w	0.2	2034.2	4320	0.0	F5
Woodpecker Trail 3442	—	1.6	2035.8	5040	4.9	F6
Russell Creek	w	2.8	2038.6	5520	1.9	F6
Jefferson Park Trail 3429	—	0.6	2039.2	5640	2.2	F6
Ford Whitewater Creek	w	0.4	2039.6	5680	1.1	F6
Spur to Scout Lake	—	0.5	2040.1	5860	3.9	F6
Spur trail to Scout and Bays lakes	—	0.3	2040.4	5930	2.5	F6
Junction with South Breitenbush Trail 3375	—	0.5	2040.9	5870	-1.3	F6
Cross South Fork Breitenbush River	w	0.1	2041.0	5840	-3.3	F6
Viewpoint	—	2.0	2043.0	6920	5.9	F6
Low saddle	—	2.1	2045.1	6150	-4.0	F7
Skyline Road 42 (4220) near Breitenbush Lake	w,R	1.6	2046.7	5500	-4.4	F7
East shore of a shallow lake	w	0.5	2047.2	5750	5.4	F7

OREGON

Landmark	Facilities	Diff	S->N	Elev	Gra	Map
Junction with old OST route, now Gibson Trail 708	—	1.0	2048.2	5510	-2.6	F7
Horseshoe Saddle Trail 712	—	0.1	2048.3	5520	1.1	F7
Ruddy Hill Trail 714	—	0.3	2048.6	5600	2.9	F7
Many Lakes Viewpoint	—	1.2	2049.8	5660	0.5	F7
Upper Lake, very good campsite	w	0.9	2050.7	5380	-3.4	F7
Cigar Lake	w	0.4	2051.1	5350	-0.8	F7
Junction to Fork Lake	—	0.4	2051.5	5280	-1.9	F7
Small triangular, semiclear lake	w	0.9	2052.4	5180	-1.2	F7
Head Lake	w	0.7	2053.1	4950	-3.6	F7
Olallie Lake Resort c/o USFS Estacada Station Attn: (Your Name) PCT Hiker 595 NW Industrial Way Estacada, OR 97023	w,G,R: 0.10m E	0.0	2053.1	4950	-3.6	F7
Skyline Road 42 (4220) near Olallie Lake Resort	R	0.1	2053.2	4990	4.3	F7
Olallie Butte Trail 720	—	2.2	2055.4	4680	-1.5	F7
Junction with old OST, known as Lodgepole Trail 706	—	1.0	2056.4	4570	-1.2	F8
Russ Lake Trail 716	—	0.3	2056.7	4550	-0.7	F8
Jude Lake	w	0.2	2056.9	4600	2.7	F8
Lemiti Creek	w	6.0	2062.9	4360	-0.4	F8
Junction to Trooper Springs	w: 0.05m SW	0.5	2063.4	4400	0.9	F8
Chinquapin Viewpoint	—	2.8	2066.2	5000	2.3	F8
Cross a saddle	—	0.8	2067.0	4980	-0.3	F9
Spur trail to view north of Mt. Hood	—	1.4	2068.4	4640	-2.6	F9
Spur trail to a seeping spring	w: 0.05m W	3.3	2071.7	3860	-2.6	F9
Cross Warm Springs River	w	2.3	2074.0	3300	-2.6	F10
Spur trail to a another spring	w: 0.05m SE	0.4	2074.4	3450	4.1	F10
Junction with Road 4245	R	1.0	2075.4	3720	2.9	F10

OREGON

Landmark	Facilities	Diff	S->N	Elev	Gra	Map
East slope of Summit Butte	—	1.7	2077.1	4230	3.3	F10
Unseen Red Wolf Pass	—	1.4	2078.5	4120	-0.9	F10
Reach a jeep road	R	0.8	2079.3	3990	-1.8	F10
Close Road S549	R	1.3	2080.6	3580	-3.4	F10
Junction with Miller Trail 534 to Clackamas Lake Campground	w: 0.30m NW	1.9	2082.5	3400	-1.0	F11
Oak Grove Fork Clackamas River	—	0.7	2083.2	3350	-0.8	F11
Skyline Road 42	R	0.2	2083.4	3370	1.1	F11
Timothy Trail 528	—	1.4	2084.8	3320	-0.4	F11
Crater Creek	w	4.3	2089.1	3220	-0.3	F11
Little Crater Lake Trail 500	w: 0.12m E	0.2	2089.3	3230	0.5	F11
Road 5890	R	1.6	2090.9	3360	0.9	F11
Jackson Meadow/Salmon River trail	—	0.9	2091.8	3680	3.9	F11
Abbot Road 58	R	0.6	2092.4	3860	3.3	F12
Linney Creek Road 240	R	0.8	2093.2	3880	0.3	F12
Pass a small campsite with seeping spring	w	0.2	2093.4	3910	1.6	F12
Climb north to a saddle	—	0.5	2093.9	4010	2.2	F12
U.S. Highway 26 at Wapinitia Pass	R	3.5	2097.4	3910	-0.3	F13
Switchback north to a near-crest junction to Twin Lakes trail	—	1.2	2098.6	4360	4.1	F13
Traverse north to a broad saddle	—	1.1	2099.7	4450	0.9	F14
Reunion with the loop trail	—	0.5	2100.2	4500	1.1	F14
Palmateer View Trail 482	—	0.5	2100.7	4550	1.1	F14
Old section of Highway 35 at Barlow Pass	R	1.5	2102.2	4157	-2.8	F14
Cross new section of Highway 35 near Barlow Pass	w,R: 0.10m E	0.2	2102.4	4155	-0.1	F14
General Delivery Government Camp, OR 97028 (503) 272-3238	PO,w,G,R: 6.00m W	0.0	2102.4	4155	-0.1	F14

OREGON

Landmark	Facilities	Diff	S->N	Elev	Gra	Map
Gully with a campsite	w	2.7	2105.1	4870	2.9	G1
Join the Timberline Trail 600	—	0.9	2106.0	5340	5.7	G1
White River Buried Forest Overlook	—	0.8	2106.8	5790	6.1	G1
Cross upper Salmon River	w	0.3	2107.1	5900	4.0	G1
Spur trail to Timberline Lodge	—	0.2	2107.3	5960	3.3	G1
Timberline Ski Area WY'East Store Attn: (Your Name) PCT Hiker 27500 East Timberline Road Timberline Lodge, OR 97028 (503) 272-3189; (503) 272-3129 $5 handling fee	w,G,M,L,r, R: 0.10m S	0.0	2107.3	5940	3.3	G1
Pass a microwave tower	—	0.2	2107.5	5980	2.2	G1
Cross Little Zigzag Creek	w	0.9	2108.4	5760	-2.7	G1
Hidden Lake Trail 779	—	0.4	2108.8	5680	-2.2	G1
Cross silty Zigzag River	w	1.3	2110.1	4890	-6.6	G1
Paradise Park Trail 778	—	0.4	2110.5	5390	13.7	G2
Lost Creek	—	0.6	2111.1	5390	0.0	G1
Rushing Water Creek	w	0.6	2111.7	5440	0.9	G2
Rejoin older PCT route	w	0.5	2112.2	5400	-0.9	G2
Scout Camp	w	3.0	2115.2	3400	-7.3	G2
Flat bench suitable for camping	w	0.3	2115.5	3270	-4.7	G3
Ramona Falls Loop Trail 797	—	0.1	2115.6	3320	5.4	G3
Junction with Trail 770	w	1.5	2117.1	2780	-3.9	G3
Trail junction, about 70 yards before Muddy Fork	—	0.5	2117.6	2800	0.4	G3
Ridge	w	1.7	2119.3	3910	7.1	G3
Junction with Timberline Trail	w	0.7	2120.0	4270	5.6	G3
End of crestline before descending north	—	1.4	2121.4	4200	-0.5	G3
Lolo Pass Road 18 at Lolo Pass	R	1.4	2122.8	3420	-6.1	G4
Trickling creek	w	0.4	2123.2	3520	2.7	G4

OREGON

Landmark	Facilities	Diff	S->N	Elev	Gra	Map
Junction with Huckleberry Mountain Trail 617 to Salvation Spring Camp	w: 0.30m N	3.9	2127.1	4020	1.4	G4
Preachers/Devils saddle	—	0.9	2128.0	4340	3.9	G4
Descend west to a notch	—	1.9	2129.9	4250	-0.5	G4
Buck Peak Trail 615	—	0.5	2130.4	4500	5.4	G4
Discover a small spring	w	0.4	2130.8	4340	-4.3	G4
Reach the ridge again	—	0.3	2131.1	4230	-4.0	G5
Reach abandoned OST	—	2.2	2133.3	4190	-0.2	G5
Larch Mountain Road 2030	R	0.1	2133.4	4240	5.4	G5
Spur of Indian Mountain with view of Mts. St. Helens, Rainier, Adams		1.6	2135.0	4400	1.1	G5
Indian Springs Campground	w	0.3	2135.3	4300	-3.6	G5
Junction with Eagle Creek Trail 440 to Wahtum Lake	w	2.6	2137.9	3750	-2.3	G5
Lateral trail to Wahtum Lake Campground	—	0.2	2138.1	3750	0.0	G5
Chinidere Mountain Trail	—	1.8	2139.9	4270	3.1	G5
Saddle to a viewpoint	—	0.6	2140.5	4140	-2.4	G5
Second saddle	—	1.4	2141.9	3830	-2.4	G6
Camp Smokey saddle, third saddle	w: 0.12m W	0.8	2142.7	3810	-0.3	G6
Benson Way Trail 405B	—	0.5	2143.2	4100	6.3	G6
Ruckel Creek Trail 405	w: 0.50m W	0.9	2144.1	4110	0.1	G7
Benson Ruckel Trail	—	0.7	2144.8	3980	-2.0	G7
Second Benson Way Trail 405B	—	0.7	2145.5	3760	-3.4	G7
Another waterless campsite	—	0.6	2146.1	3680	-1.4	G7
Teakettle Spring	w	0.3	2146.4	3360	-12.0	G7
Junction to Columbia Gorge Work Center, lateral trail to Herman Creek		3.0	2149.4	1120	-8.1	G7
Cross a creek	w	0.5	2149.9	960	-3.5	G7

OREGON

Landmark	Facilities	Diff	S->N	Elev	Gra	Map
Misnamed Dry Creek, camping possible	w	1.8	2151.7	720	-1.4	G7
Powerline road	R	0.7	2152.4	680	-0.6	G7
SE Undine Street	—	1.0	2153.4	240	-4.8	G7
General Delivery Cascade Locks, OR 97014 (541) 374-5026	PO,w,G,M,L,sh,r, R: 0.25m NE	0.0	2153.4	240	-4.8	G7
Bridge of the Gods, east end	—	0.1	2153.5	200	-4.3	G7

Oregon

WASHINGTON

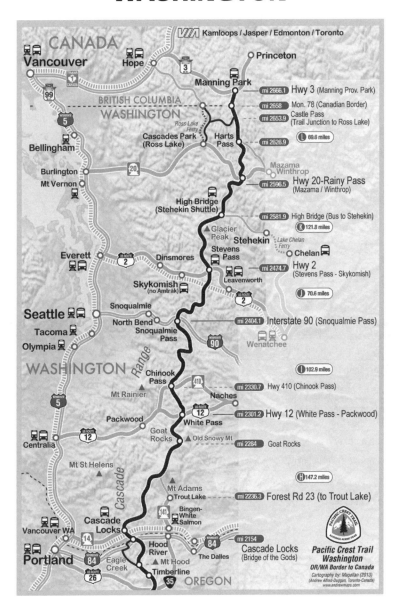

CANADA

🚌🚌 Vancouver

Kamloops / Jasper / Edmonton / Toronto

🚌🚌 Hope

O Princeton

3

Manning Park

mi 2666.1 Hwy 3 (Manning Prov. Park)

99

BRITISH COLUMBIA
WASHINGTON

5

Ross Lake
Ferry

mi 2658 Mon. 78 (Canadian Border)

mi 2653.9 Castle Pass
(Trail Junction to Ross Lake)

69.6 miles

Bellingham

Cascades Park
(Ross Lake)

Harts
Pass

mi 2626.9

Burlington
Mt Vernon

20

Mazama
Winthrop

mi 2596.5 Hwy 20-Rainy Pass
(Mazama / Winthrop)

High Bridge
(Stehekin Shuttle)

mi 2581.9 High Bridge (Bus to Stehekin)

121.8 miles

▲Glacier
Peak

Stehekin

Lake Chelan
Ferry

O Chelan 🚌

Everett 🚌🚌

Dinsmores

Stevens
Pass

mi 2474.7 Hwy 2
(Stevens Pass - Skykomish)

Leavenworth

Skykomish
(no Amtrak)🚌

2

70.6 miles

Seattle 🚌🚌

Snoqualmie

Tacoma 🚌
Olympia 🚌

North Bend
Snoqualmie
Pass

mi 2404.1 Interstate 90 (Snoqualmie Pass)

90

Wenatchee

WASHINGTON Range

102.9 miles

Chinook
Pass

410

mi 2330.7 Hwy 410 (Chinook Pass)

Mt Rainier

Naches

5

12
White Pass

mi 2301.2 Hwy 12 (White Pass - Packwood)

Packwood

Goat
Rocks

🚌🚌 Centralia

12

▲ Old Snowy Mt

mi 2284 Goat Rocks

Mt St Helens
▲

Cascade

147.2 miles

▲
Mt Adams
O Trout Lake

mi 2236.3 Forest Rd 23 (to Trout Lake)

Bingen-
White
🚊Salmon

141

🚌🚌 Vancouver WA

Cascade
Locks

14

84

mi 2154

Portland 🚌🚌

84

Eagle
Creek

Hood
River

26

▲ Mt Hood

Timberline

The Dalles

Cascade Locks
(Bridge of the Gods)

35

OREGON

PACIFIC CREST TRAIL
NATIONAL SCENIC TRAIL

Pacific Crest Trail
Washington
OR/WA Border to Canada
Cartography by: Magellan (2013)
(Andrew Alfred-Duggan, Toronto-Canada)
www.andrewmaps.com

Washington

WASHINGTON

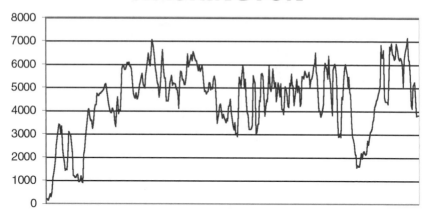

**Elevation Profile for Washington
From Oregon-Washington Border to Canada**

Section Total Mileage: 512.6 miles

Landmark	Facilities	Diff	S->N	Elev	Gra	Map
Bridge of the Gods, west end	—	0.5	2154.0	200	0.0	H1
PCT trailhead	—	0.2	2154.2	150	-2.7	H1
Cross a paved road	R	0.8	2155.0	140	-0.1	H1
Climb to a ridge, meet Tamehnous Trail 25	—	0.4	2155.4	250	3.0	H1
Reach a utility road	R	2.1	2157.5	410	0.8	H1
Junction to Gillette Lake	w: 0.10m E	0.3	2157.8	280	-4.7	H1
Bridge across Greenleaf Creek	w	0.9	2158.7	510	2.8	H2
Low ridgecrest	—	1.9	2160.6	1100	3.4	H2
Cross a road	R	0.6	2161.2	1300	3.6	H2
Recross road	w,R: 0.20m N	0.3	2161.5	1600	10.9	H2
Water Alert (↓): 12.8m						
Southwest up to a larger ridge	—	0.9	2162.4	1970	4.5	H2

WASHINGTON

Landmark	Facilities	Diff	S->N	Elev	Gra	Map
Viewpoint, spring near Table Mountain	—	1.3	2163.7	2480	4.3	H2
Nearby road	R	0.8	2164.5	2790	4.2	H2
Ridge above a powerline saddle	—	0.5	2165.0	3120	7.2	H2
Climb to a saddle and cross it, first view of Three Corner Rock	—	0.7	2165.7	3400	4.3	H2
Come to a seep, maybe dry	—	0.3	2166.0	3370	-1.1	H2
Crestline road	R	1.3	2167.3	3020	-2.9	H2
Spur trail to Three Corner Rock water trough, has a leak	—	2.0	2169.3	3320	1.6	H3
Viewless saddle by Road 2090	R	1.9	2171.2	2360	-5.5	H3
Crest gap	—	0.5	2171.7	1980	-8.3	H4
Road 2000	R	1.8	2173.5	1720	-1.6	H4
Rock Creek	w	0.8	2174.3	1420	-4.1	H4
Water Alert (↑): 13.0m						
Snag Creek	w	0.4	2174.7	1470	1.4	H4
Road 2070	w,R: 0.12m SE	0.3	2175.0	1450	-0.7	H4
Seasonal creeklet	w	1.8	2176.8	2080	3.8	H4
South-trending ridge	—	1.8	2178.6	3080	6.0	H4
Second saddle, almost touch Road 41	R	0.7	2179.3	2985	-1.5	H4
Cross Sunset-Hemlock Road 41	R	0.8	2180.1	2950	-0.5	H4
Forest to main ridge	—	1.0	2181.1	2550	-4.3	H4
Northeast down to a viewless saddle	—	0.7	2181.8	2150	-6.2	H4
Cross a wide, splashing tributary of Trout Creek	w	2.0	2183.8	1210	-5.1	H4
Cross Road 43 alongside Trout Creek	R	0.3	2184.1	1180	-1.1	H5
Southeast to Road 417	R	0.8	2184.9	1120	-0.8	H5
Junction to Wind River Ranger Station	—	0.1	2185.0	1120	0.0	H5

WASHINGTON

Landmark	Facilities	Diff	S->N	Elev	Gra	Map
Bunker Hill Trail	—	0.5	2185.5	1210	2.0	H5
Cross a crest	—	0.7	2186.2	1250	0.6	H5
Little Soda Springs Road 54	R	0.8	2187.0	940	-4.2	H5
Cross Wind River	w	0.3	2187.3	940	0.0	H5
Wind River Road	R	0.2	2187.5	1020	4.3	H5
Cross Road 6517	R	0.8	2188.3	1180	2.2	H5
Down to Panther Creek Road 65	R	1.2	2189.5	930	-2.3	H5
Panther Creek	w	0.2	2189.7	900	-1.6	H5
Westernmost end of a ridge	—	2.1	2191.8	2100	6.2	H6
Saddle where a good dirt road starts	R	1.1	2192.9	2300	2.0	H6
Junction with Road 68	R	1.3	2194.2	2810	4.3	H6
Descend to a broad, open saddle	—	1.7	2195.9	3214	2.6	H6
Junction to Cedar Creek, about 350 feet drop	w: 0.30m S	1.1	2197.0	3550	3.3	H7
Junction with the old Cascade Crest Trail	—	1.0	2198.0	4000	4.9	H7
Junction with the Big Huckle-berry Mountain summit trail	—	0.1	2198.1	4010	1.1	H7
Second saddle	—	1.3	2199.4	3730	-2.3	H7
Descend to a gully that has a reliable spring	w	0.5	2199.9	3550	-3.9	H7
Reach a viewless, broad saddle	—	0.8	2200.7	3580	0.4	H7
Head towards Road 6801	R	0.8	2201.5	3220	-4.9	H7
Road 60, back of Crest Campground	R	3.5	2205.0	3490	0.8	H8
Duck pond named as Sheep Lake	w	1.9	2206.9	4020	3.0	H8
Green Lake	w	1.1	2208.0	4250	2.3	H8
Junction with Shortcut Trail 171A	—	0.4	2208.4	4240	-0.3	H8

WASHINGTON

Landmark	Facilities	Diff	S->N	Elev	Gra	Map
Switchback to a saddle	—	2.9	2211.3	4730	1.8	H8
Outlet creek of Lake Sebago	w	0.9	2212.2	4640	-1.1	H8
Blue Lake	w	0.2	2212.4	4630	-0.5	H8
Junction with East Crater Trail 48	w	1.9	2214.3	4730	0.6	H9
Meet Lemei Lake Trail 33A	w	0.1	2214.4	4730	0.0	H9
Bear Lake, Elk Lake Trail 176	w	1.0	2215.4	4790	0.7	H9
Slope above east end of Deer Lake	w	0.4	2215.8	4830	1.1	H9
Indian Heaven Trail 33	—	0.1	2215.9	4880	5.4	H9
Placid Lake Trail 29	—	1.1	2217.0	4980	1.0	H9
Second saddle to a campsite	—	0.5	2217.5	5110	2.8	H9
West end of Cultus Creek Trail 108	—	0.4	2217.9	5150	1.1	H9
Junction to Sawtooth Mountain, south end	—	1.2	2219.1	4850	-2.7	H9
Junction to Sawtooth Mountain, north end	—	1.4	2220.5	4570	-2.2	H9
Cross Road 24	R	1.2	2221.7	4260	-2.8	H9
Descend to a saddle	—	1.4	2223.1	4070	-1.5	H10
Road 8851	R	2.5	2225.6	3915	-0.7	H10
Outlet of Big Mosquito Lake	w	0.1	2225.7	3900	-1.6	H10
Cross a dirt road	R	2.4	2228.1	4090	0.9	H10
Steamboat Lake spur trail	w	0.4	2228.5	3980	-3.0	H10
End of the alternate trail, climbs to Steamboat Lake Campground		0.8	2229.3	3970	-0.1	H11
Junction with Road 88	R	1.2	2230.5	3470	-4.5	H11
Trout Lake Creek	w	0.4	2230.9	3310	-4.3	H11
Road 8810	R	2.1	2233.0	4140	4.3	H12
Reach the crest	—	0.6	2233.6	4570	7.8	H12

WASHINGTON

Landmark	Facilities	Diff	S->N	Elev	Gra	Map
Road 23, trailhead at Road 8810	w,R	2.7	2236.3	3854	-2.9	H12
Road 521	R	0.9	2237.2	4020	2.0	H12
Swampy Creek	w	0.3	2237.5	4020	0.0	H12
Spring, 100 yards past White Salmon River	w	2.4	2239.9	4900	4.0	H12
Junction with Stagman Ridge Trail 12	—	2.5	2242.4	5790	3.9	H13
Junction with Round the Mountain Trail 9	—	0.5	2242.9	5900	2.4	H13
Traverse to a saddle, east of Burnt Rock	—	3.2	2246.1	5950	0.2	H13
Sheep Lake	w	0.3	2246.4	5768	-6.6	H13
Cross Riley Creek	w	0.2	2246.6	5770	0.1	H13
Mutton Creek	w	1.3	2247.9	5900	1.1	H13
Cross Lewis River	w	1.3	2249.2	6060	1.3	H13
Junction with Divide Camp Trail 112	w	0.3	2249.5	6020	-1.4	H13
Junction with Killen Creek Trail 113	w	1.4	2250.9	6084	0.5	H14
Cross Killen Creek	w	0.8	2251.7	5920	-2.2	H14
Highline Trail 114	—	0.2	2251.9	5900	-1.1	H14
Readily accessible second pond, first one better	w	0.4	2252.3	5772	-3.5	H14
Trail to junction with Highline Trail	—	2.0	2254.3	5231	-2.9	H14
Cross Muddy Fork	w	1.6	2255.9	4740	-3.3	H14
Westward to a very good campsite	w	0.5	2256.4	4590	-3.3	H14
Trailside Lava Spring	w	0.3	2256.7	4520	-2.5	H14
Road 5603	R	1.6	2258.3	4750	1.6	H14
East-west road near Midway site, junction with Road 115	R	2.0	2260.3	4490	-1.4	H15

WASHINGTON

Landmark	Facilities	Diff	S->N	Elev	Gra	Map
Closed Road 655	R	0.1	2260.4	4520	3.3	H15
Cross Midway Creek	w	0.4	2260.8	4690	4.6	H15
Leave last pond	w	2.8	2263.6	5070	1.5	H15
Climb to a switchback	—	1.6	2265.2	5220	1.0	H15
Climb to a saddle, pass 2 small ponds	—	0.7	2265.9	5450	3.6	H15
Prominent ridgecrest	—	0.8	2266.7	5600	2.0	H16
Cross a trickling creek	w	1.4	2268.1	5140	-3.6	H16
50-yard pond	w	0.5	2268.6	5050	-2.0	H16
Walupt Lake Trail 101	—	3.4	2272.0	4960	-0.3	H17
Walupt Creek	w	3.9	2275.9	5480	1.4	H17
Sheep Lake near Nannie Ridge Trail 98	w	0.6	2276.5	5760	5.1	H17
Crest saddle	—	1.4	2277.9	6100	2.6	H17
Cispus Pass	—	0.9	2278.8	6460	4.3	H17
Campsite beside easternmost tributary of Cispus River	w	0.6	2279.4	6130	-6.0	H17
Junction with Trail 97 to Bypass Camp	w: 0.60m W	1.6	2281.0	5930	-1.4	H17
Trail 96 junction	—	1.0	2282.0	6420	5.3	H17
Dana May Yelverton Shelter, may be unsafe, broken	—	1.1	2283.1	7040	6.1	H18
Down to crest saddle	—	1.0	2284.1	6850	-2.1	H18
Upper end of Coyote Trail 79	—	1.3	2285.4	6680	-1.4	H18
Bleak, alpine campsites	w	0.3	2285.7	6320	-13.0	H18
Saddle, former Cascade Crest Trail drops southeast	—	1.3	2287.0	5820	-4.2	H18
Almost touches a crest saddle	—	0.6	2287.6	5580	-4.3	H18
Junction with the old CCT	—	0.5	2288.1	5200	-8.3	H18
Saddle that holds Lutz Lake and small campsites	w	0.6	2288.7	5100	-1.8	H18

Washington

WASHINGTON

Landmark	Facilities	Diff	S->N	Elev	Gra	Map
Tieton Pass	—	1.0	2289.7	4570	-5.8	H19
Cross east over the divide	—	1.5	2291.2	4930	2.6	H19
Junction with Trail 1117 to Hidden Spring	w: 0.30m E	1.8	2293.0	5520	3.6	H19
West on a mid 80s segment	—	0.9	2293.9	6040	6.3	H19
Top a narrow ridge	—	1.2	2295.1	6620	5.3	H19
Junction with Chairlift Trail	—	2.5	2297.6	5830	-3.4	H19
Junction with Hogback Trail 1144	—	1.2	2298.8	5400	-3.9	H19
Ginnette Lake	w	0.2	2299.0	5400	0.0	H19
US Highway 12 (old state Highway 14) near White Pass	R	2.2	2301.2	4405	-4.9	H19
White Pass P.O. (The Kracker Barrel Store) Attn: (Your Name) PCT Hiker 48851 US Highway 12 Naches, WA 98937 (509) 672-3105	PO,w,G,M,sh,r,R: 0.70m W	0.0	2301.2	4405	-4.9	H19
Start from the parking lot	—	0.2	2301.4	4415	0.5	I1
Junction with Dark Meadows Trail 1107	w	1.1	2302.5	4780	3.6	I1
Deer Lake	w	1.0	2303.5	5206	4.6	I1
Sand Lake	w	0.5	2304.0	5295	1.9	I1
Cortright Creek Trail 57	—	2.0	2306.0	5520	1.2	I1
Buesch Lake	w	1.1	2307.1	5081	-4.3	I1
Good picnic spot next to a slender lake	w	1.1	2308.2	5180	1.0	I1
Cowlitz Pass	—	0.5	2308.7	5160	-0.4	I1
Cowlitz Trail 44	—	0.2	2308.9	5140	-1.1	I1
Snow Lake	—	2.1	2311.0	4935	-1.1	I2
Pothole Trail 45	—	0.8	2311.8	4900	-0.5	I2
Packer campsite	w	2.9	2314.7	4620	-1.0	I2

WASHINGTON

Landmark	Facilities	Diff	S->N	Elev	Gra	Map
Bumping River ford by Bumping Lake Trail, Fish Lake	w	1.1	2315.8	4100	-5.1	I3
Reliable drinkable rill	w	2.7	2318.5	5170	4.3	I3
Laughingwater Trail 22	—	1.6	2320.1	5690	3.5	I3
Trail 380 to Two Lakes	w: 0.30m SE	1.6	2321.7	5660	-0.2	I3
American Ridge Trail 958	—	2.6	2324.3	5320	-1.4	I4
Anderson Lake	w	1.4	2325.7	5340	0.2	I4
Dewey Lake	w	1.8	2327.5	5112	-1.4	I4
Dewey Lake Trail 968	w	0.5	2328.0	5130	0.4	I4
Highway 410 at Chinook Pass	w,R: 0.33m S	2.7	2330.7	5432	1.2	I5
Sheep Lake	w	2.2	2332.9	5750	1.6	I5
Sourdough Gap	—	1.2	2334.1	6440	6.3	I6
Meet Silver Creek Trail 1192	—	2.1	2336.2	5882	-2.9	I6
Obscure trail signed FOG CITY and GOLD HILL	—	1.1	2337.3	6040	1.6	I6
Meet 2 trails, to Gold Hill and to Union Creek Trail 956	—	0.3	2337.6	6200	5.8	I6
Blue Bell Pass	—	0.4	2338.0	6390	5.2	I6
Bullion Basin Trail 1156	—	0.9	2338.9	6150	-2.9	I6
Scout Pass	—	1.5	2340.4	6530	2.8	I6
Junction to Basin Lake, excellent camping	w: 0.50m SE	0.6	2341.0	6390	-2.5	I6
Big Crow Basin Spring near Norse Peak Trail, reliable spring	w	0.4	2341.4	6290	-2.7	I6
Barnard Saddle	—	0.8	2342.2	6150	-1.9	I7
Hayden Pass	—	0.3	2342.5	6150	0.0	I7
Sign LITTLE CROW BASIN	w: 0.10m S	0.4	2342.9	5930	-6.0	I7
Martinson Gap	—	1.4	2344.3	5720	-1.6	I7
Arch Rock Way 1187	—	2.1	2346.4	5930	1.1	I8
Unsigned spur to Morgan Springs	w: 0.25m E	0.5	2346.9	5700	-5.0	I8

WASHINGTON

Landmark	Facilities	Diff	S->N	Elev	Gra	Map
Cougar Valley Trail	—	0.3	2347.2	5780	2.9	I9
Junction to summit	—	0.5	2347.7	5920	3.0	I9
Spur trail to Arch Rock shelter	w: 0.10m W	0.8	2348.5	5760	-2.2	I9
Louisiana Saddle	—	1.5	2350.0	5220	-3.9	I9
Rods Gap	—	1.1	2351.1	4820	-3.9	I9
Maggie Way Trail 1186	—	1.6	2352.7	4850	0.2	I9
Camp Urich at Government Meadow	w	0.8	2353.5	4750	-1.4	I10
Cross historic road	R	0.2	2353.7	4780	1.6	I10
Road bends southwest	R	1.1	2354.8	4840	0.6	I10
Pyramid Peak Trail Junction	—	0.4	2355.2	5000	4.3	I10
Windy Gap	—	1.0	2356.2	5200	2.2	I10
Cross a road to a spring	w,R	2.4	2358.6	5020	-0.8	I10
Water Alert (↓): 22.1m						
Descend to another road	R	1.0	2359.6	4640	-4.1	I11
Road-laced crest saddle	R	1.4	2361.0	4900	2.0	I11
Cross Road 784	R	1.3	2362.3	4920	0.2	I11
West Fork Bear Creek Trail	—	1.0	2363.3	5340	4.6	I11
Granite Creek Trail 1326 on Blowout Mountain, see map for alternate route for water	w: 0.70m NE	1.0	2364.3	5480	1.5	I11
Blowout Mountain Trail 1318	—	1.1	2365.4	5260	-2.2	I11
Cross 2 roads to a major saddle	R	2.8	2368.2	4400	-3.3	I12
Tacoma Pass	—	2.7	2370.9	3460	-3.8	I12
Sheets Pass	—	1.4	2372.3	3720	2.0	I12
Seasonal creek, good to mid-August only on a wet year	—	0.4	2372.7	3860	3.8	I12
Broad saddle littered with blowdowns	—	3.8	2376.5	4200	1.0	I12
Low point of the pass	—	2.3	2378.8	4290	0.4	I13

WASHINGTON

Landmark	Facilities	Diff	S->N	Elev	Gra	Map
Cross weather station access road	w,R: 0.10m W	1.8	2380.6	3950	-2.1	I13
Water Alert (↑): 22.0m						
Stampede Pass Road 54, junction to Lizard Lake	w,R: 0.20m S	1.0	2381.6	3680	-2.9	I13
Trail follows to a hairpin on a road	R	2.1	2383.7	3840	0.8	I14
Dandy Pass	—	0.3	2384.0	3680	-5.8	I14
Come to a creek	w	1.9	2385.9	3600	-0.5	I14
Stirrup Creek	w	0.8	2386.7	3480	-1.6	I14
Headwaters of Meadow Creek	—	2.1	2388.8	3660	0.9	I14
West shore of Twilight Lake	w	1.4	2390.2	3575	-0.7	I14
Mirror Lake	w	0.9	2391.1	4195	7.5	I15
Mirror Lake Trail 1302	—	0.4	2391.5	4220	0.7	I15
Drop north from sign COLD CREEK TRAIL	—	0.5	2392.0	4500	6.1	I15
Descend to a perennial creek	w: 0.05m W	2.5	2394.5	3900	-2.6	I15
Olallie Creek	w	0.8	2395.3	3620	-3.8	I15
Powerline access road	R	0.7	2396.0	3350	-4.2	I15
Lodge Lake	w	2.0	2398.0	3180	-0.9	I15
Beaver Lake	w	0.8	2398.8	3480	4.1	I15
Trailhead parking area south of I-90	—	1.0	2399.8	3030	-4.9	I15
Highway 906	R	0.3	2400.1	3000	-1.1	I15
Chevron Gas Station Attn: (Your Name) PCT Hiker 521 State Route 906 Snoqualmie Pass, WA 98068 (425) 434-6688	w,G,M,L, R: 0.20m SE	0.0	2400.1	3000	-1.1	I15

Washington

WASHINGTON

Landmark	Facilities	Diff	S->N	Elev	Gra	Map
Summit Inn Attn: (Your Name) PCT Hiker 603 State Route 906 P.O. Box 163 Snoqualmie Pass, WA 98068 (425) 434-6300 $15 + tax if not staying	w,G,M,L,r, R: 0.20m SE	0.0	2400.1	3000	-1.1	I15
Interstate 90 at Snoqualmie Pass	R	0.1	2400.2	3000	0.0	I15
Northbound Trailhead parking lot north of I-90	R	0.2	2400.4	3080	4.3	J1
Red Mountain trail 1033	w: 0.30m N	2.5	2402.9	3820	3.2	J1
Cross east side of the crest	—	3.2	2406.1	5440	5.5	J1
Crest saddle between Ridge and Gravel lakes	w	1.1	2407.2	5270	-1.7	J1
Forested saddle between Joe and Edds lakes	—	2.2	2409.4	5030	-1.2	J1
Huckleberry Saddle	—	1.5	2410.9	5560	3.8	J2
Needle Sight Gap	—	0.6	2411.5	5930	6.7	J2
Chikamin Pass	—	2.5	2414.0	5780	-0.7	J2
Spur to more campsites near Park Lakes	w	1.4	2415.4	4960	-6.4	J2
Spur of Three Queens	—	0.8	2416.2	5350	5.3	J2
Spectacle Lake Trail 1306	—	1.6	2417.8	4440	-6.2	J2
Delate Creek, has a campsite	w	1.2	2419.0	3920	-4.7	J2
Small campsite	w	0.3	2419.3	3800	-4.3	J2
Pete Lake Trail 1323	—	1.8	2421.1	3210	-3.6	J2
Lemah Creek	w	0.8	2421.9	3200	-0.1	J2
Lemah Meadow Trail 1323B	w	0.7	2422.6	3210	0.2	J2
A couple of campsites	w	0.1	2422.7	3240	3.3	J2
Switchback out of Lemah Creek	w: 0.25m NW	0.7	2423.4	3370	2.0	J2
Secluded cirque with a chilly tarn	w	5.3	2428.7	5520	4.4	J3

Washington

WASHINGTON

Landmark	Facilities	Diff	S->N	Elev	Gra	Map
Cross the inlet	w	1.3	2430.0	5300	-1.8	J4
Waptus Burn Trail 1329C	—	1.7	2431.7	5180	-0.8	J3
Dutch Miller Gap Trail 1362	—	4.7	2436.4	3050	-4.9	J4
Waptus River	w	0.1	2436.5	3020	-3.3	J4
Waptus River Trail 1310	w	0.8	2437.3	3070	0.7	J4
Second stream with campsite near Spade Lake Trail 1337	w	1.5	2438.8	3400	2.4	J4
Spinola Creek Trail 1310A	—	1.1	2439.9	3440	0.4	J5
Lake Vicente Trail 1365	—	3.8	2443.7	4440	2.9	J6
Deep Lake's campsite access trail	w	0.5	2444.2	4400	-0.9	J6
Trail 1375	—	3.0	2447.2	5560	4.2	J6
Cathedral Pass	—	0.2	2447.4	5610	2.7	J6
Few small tarns	—	0.1	2447.5	5460	-17.0	J6
Junction of 2 streams	w	2.0	2449.5	4600	-4.7	J6
Cross second creek carefully, drains Mt. Daniel's NE slopes	w	1.4	2450.9	3770	-6.4	J6
Cross headwaters of Cle Elum drainage where trail turns East	w	1.0	2451.9	4180	4.5	J6
Deception Pass	—	0.8	2452.7	4470	3.9	J6
Cross a stream near a campsite	w	1.9	2454.6	4400	-0.4	J6
Cross outlet of Deception Lakes	w	1.5	2456.1	5040	4.6	J7
Pieper Pass	—	2.0	2458.1	5920	4.8	J7
Glacier Lake campsite, past a campsite	w	2.0	2460.1	5000	-5.0	J7
Surprise Lake Trail 1060	w	0.8	2460.9	4840	-2.2	J7
Trap Pass Trail 1060A	—	1.0	2461.9	5080	2.6	J7
Trap Pass	—	0.9	2462.8	5800	8.7	J7
Access trail to Trap Lake	—	0.8	2463.6	5350	-6.1	J8
Campsite beside a seasonal creek	w	1.2	2464.8	4970	-3.4	J8

Washington

WASHINGTON

Landmark	Facilities	Diff	S->N	Elev	Gra	Map
Climb to a notch	—	0.7	2465.5	5210	3.7	J8
Hope Lake	w	1.1	2466.6	4400	-8.0	J8
North end of Mig Lake	w	0.7	2467.3	4670	4.2	J8
Unnamed crest saddle	—	1.8	2469.1	5190	3.1	J8
Josephine Lake's cirque	—	0.8	2469.9	4980	-2.8	J8
North shore of Lake Susan Jane	w	0.5	2470.4	4600	-8.3	J8
Saddle near the top of a chairlift	—	2.2	2472.6	5160	2.8	J8
Highway 2 at Stevens Pass, parking area	R	2.1	2474.7	4060	-5.7	J8
General Delivery Skykomish, WA 98288 (360) 677-2241	PO,w,G,M,L,r, R: 14.00m W	0.0	2474.7	4060	-5.7	J8
3-yard-wide tributary of Nason Creek	w	2.5	2477.2	3850	-0.9	K1
Meadow where Nason Creek flows	w	1.0	2478.2	4220	4.0	K1
Switchback up to a saddle	—	1.7	2479.9	5030	5.2	K1
Spur trail to Lake Valhalla	w	0.3	2480.2	4900	-4.7	K1
Smithbrook Trail 1590	—	1.8	2482.0	4700	-1.2	K1
Delightful cascade	w	1.8	2483.8	4200	-3.0	K2
Lake Janus	w	0.4	2484.2	4150	-1.4	K2
Reach a crest	—	1.6	2485.8	5180	7.0	K2
Meadow with faint trail to Glasses Lake	—	0.8	2486.6	5070	-1.5	K3
West shoulder of Grizzly Peak	—	2.1	2488.7	5580	2.6	K3
Cross the crest above Grizzly Lake	—	1.4	2490.1	5120	-3.6	K3
Shadeless campsite	—	0.2	2490.3	5030	-4.9	K3
Wenatchee Pass	—	1.0	2491.3	4230	-8.7	K3
Junction with Top Lake Trail 1506	—	0.6	2491.9	4570	6.2	K4
Trail 1057 to Pear Lake's cirque	w	0.7	2492.6	4880	4.8	K4

WASHINGTON

Landmark	Facilities	Diff	S->N	Elev	Gra	Map
Up to the crest	—	1.6	2494.2	5350	3.2	K4
Fairly reliable creeks	w	2.4	2496.6	4800	-2.5	K4
Saddle Gap	—	0.7	2497.3	5060	4.0	K4
Junction with West Cady Ridge Trail 1054	—	0.3	2497.6	4930	-4.7	K4
Pass Creek Trail 1053, next to 10-foot-wide Pass Creek	w	1.0	2498.6	4200	-7.9	K4
Cady Pass	—	0.4	2499.0	4310	3.0	K4
Switchback to a crest	—	1.9	2500.9	5470	6.6	K4
Lake Sally Ann	w	1.7	2502.6	5479	0.1	K5
Junction with Cady Ridge Trail 1532	—	0.4	2503.0	5380	-2.7	K5
Wards Pass	—	0.7	2503.7	5710	5.1	K5
Bald Eagle Trail 650	—	0.6	2504.3	5600	-2.0	K5
Ridgecrest campsite	—	0.5	2504.8	5450	-3.3	K5
Junction with Little Wenatchee River Trail 1525	—	0.3	2505.1	5440	-0.4	K5
Spur trail to Trail 1525	—	0.2	2505.3	5500	3.3	K5
Kodak Peak's east ridge	—	0.7	2506.0	5660	2.5	K5
Indian Pass	—	1.3	2507.3	5020	-5.4	K5
Murky Kid Pond	w	1.0	2508.3	5320	3.3	K6
Lower White Pass	—	0.7	2509.0	5378	0.9	K6
Semi-clear Reflection Pond	w	0.3	2509.3	5560	6.6	K6
Junction at White Pass	—	1.9	2511.2	5904	2.0	K7
North Fork Sauk Trail 649	—	0.6	2511.8	5950	0.8	K7
Red Pass	—	1.3	2513.1	6500	4.6	K7
Descend to a lone, 3-foot-high cairn	—	1.4	2514.5	5700	-6.2	K7
Campsite at a saddle	—	0.3	2514.8	5500	-7.3	K7
Last crossing of a swelling creek	w	1.5	2516.3	4700	-5.8	K7

WASHINGTON

Landmark	Facilities	Diff	S->N	Elev	Gra	Map
Cross White Chuck River	w	1.0	2517.3	4000	-7.6	K7
Baekos Creek	w	1.0	2518.3	3990	-0.1	K7
Chetwok Creek	w	1.3	2519.6	3730	-2.2	K7
Sitkum Creek, excellent campsite with pit toilet	w	0.8	2520.4	3852	1.7	K8
Kennedy Creek	w	1.2	2521.6	4050	1.8	K8
Junction with Kennedy Ridge Trail 643A (Do not take this trail for exit.)	—	0.4	2522.0	4300	6.8	K8
Glacier Creek, excellent campsite	w	1.9	2523.9	5640	7.7	K8
Junction with Glacier Ridge Trail 658	—	0.7	2524.6	6050	6.4	K8
Cross Pumice Creek	w	0.5	2525.1	5900	-3.3	K8
Contour over to a ridge	—	1.6	2526.7	5770	-0.9	K8
Cross Fire Creek	w	0.8	2527.5	5370	-5.4	K8
Fire Creek Pass	—	1.7	2529.2	6350	6.3	K8
Outlet of Mica Lake	w	1.1	2530.3	5430	-9.1	K8
Open campsite by a small bench, next to Mica Creek	w	0.5	2530.8	5110	-7.0	K8
Good campsite	w	1.1	2531.9	4400	-7.0	K8
Milk Creek Trail 790 by Milk Creek	w	1.3	2533.2	3800	-5.0	K8
Reach a ridgecrest, campsite	—	2.5	2535.7	5750	8.5	K9
Small knoll	—	1.5	2537.2	5860	0.8	K9
Another ridge	—	0.6	2537.8	6010	2.7	K9
Dolly Vista campsite	w	0.7	2538.5	5830	-2.8	K9
Saddle on Vista Ridge	—	0.5	2539.0	5380	-9.8	K9
Signed campsite beside Vista Creek	w	2.6	2541.6	3650	-7.2	K10
Vista Creek	w	2.1	2543.7	2877	-4.0	K10

WASHINGTON

Landmark	Facilities	Diff	S->N	Elev	Gra	Map
Note trail to new bridge, go northwest (See New Suiattle River Bridge Map p. 116.)	—	0.0	2543.7	2877	-4.0	K10
New Suiattle River Bridge	w	3.0	2546.7	2320	-2.0	K10
East-West Suiattle River Trail 784, go east	—	0.3	2547.0	2520	7.3	K10
Suiattle River access trail	w	3.2	2550.2	2860	1.2	K10
End of trail from new bridge (See New Suiattle River Bridge Map p. 116.)	—	0.0	2550.2	2860	1.2	K10
Buck Creek Pass trail	—	4.4	2554.6	4580	4.2	K11
Miners Creek	w	0.5	2555.1	4490	-2.0	K11
Junction with old PCT route	—	1.5	2556.6	5280	5.7	K11
Spur trail to 2-tent site	—	0.7	2557.3	5790	7.9	K11
Reach Suiattle Pass with abandoned trail that goes east	—	0.3	2557.6	5990	7.3	K11
Down to a creeklet	w	0.3	2557.9	5730	-9.4	K11
Junction with Railroad Creek Trail	—	0.2	2558.1	5550	-9.8	K11
First downhill to a canyon	w	1.3	2559.4	4980	-4.8	K11
Spur trail to a 1-tent site	w	1.4	2560.8	5450	3.6	K11
Spur trail to a 2-tent site	w	1.6	2562.4	4810	-4.3	K11
Spur trail to some tent sites	w	0.2	2562.6	4680	-7.1	K11
Hemlock Camp	w	2.0	2564.6	3560	-6.1	K12
Spruce Creek Camp	w	2.7	2567.3	2900	-2.7	K12
Swamp Creek Camp	w	1.3	2568.6	2780	-1.0	K12
South Fork Agnes Creek	w	1.6	2570.2	2570	-1.4	K12
Junction with West Fork Agnes Creek Trail 1272, Five Mile Camp	w	1.4	2571.6	2160	-3.2	K12
Seasonal Trapper Creek	w	1.2	2572.8	2070	-0.8	K13
Agnes Creek	w	3.6	2576.4	1550	-1.6	K14

WASHINGTON

Landmark	Facilities	Diff	S->N	Elev	Gra	Map
Stehekin River Road	R	0.2	2576.6	1650	5.4	K14
High Bridge Ranger Station		0.1	2576.7	1600	-5.4	K14
General Delivery Stehekin, WA 98852 (509) 682-2625	PO,w,G,M,L,sh,r, R: 10.60m E	0.0	2576.7	1600	-5.4	K14
Junction to Cascade Corral	—	0.4	2577.1	1860	7.1	K14
Coon Lake	w	0.7	2577.8	2180	5.0	K14
Junction with Old Wagon Trail	—	0.8	2578.6	1940	-3.3	K14
McGregor Creek	w	0.6	2579.2	2195	4.6	K14
Buzzard Creek	w	0.4	2579.6	2260	1.8	K14
Canim Creek	w	0.7	2580.3	2160	-1.6	K14
Bridge Creek Ranger Station	w	1.3	2581.6	2105	-0.5	K14
PCT Bridge Creek trailhead on Stehekin River road	R	0.3	2581.9	2180	2.7	K14
Cross Berry Creek	w	1.7	2583.6	2720	3.4	K14
Bridge Creek	w	1.0	2584.6	2540	-2.0	K14
Junction with North Fork Bridge Creek Trail 1233	—	0.3	2584.9	2810	9.8	K14
Maple Creek	w	1.5	2586.4	3070	1.9	K14
Spur trail to Six Mile Camp	w: 0.13m SE	1.7	2588.1	3130	0.4	K14
Rainbow Lake Trail	—	0.7	2588.8	3240	1.7	K15
Spur trail to the loveliest Bridge Creek campsite: Hide-Away Camp	w: 0.10m SW	1.5	2590.3	3510	2.0	K15
Junction with Twisp Pass Trail 1277	w	0.9	2591.2	3635	1.5	K15
Stiletto Peak Trail 1232	—	1.4	2592.6	4250	4.8	K15
North Cascades National Park Boundary	—	0.5	2593.1	4180	-1.5	K15
Old PCT Route rejoins (Trail 419)	—	1.0	2594.1	4300	1.3	K15

WASHINGTON

Landmark	Facilities	Diff	S->N	Elev	Gra	Map
Spur trail to Highway 20 parking lot	—	0.9	2595.0	4510	2.5	K16
Rainy Lake's outlet creek	w	0.5	2595.5	4705	4.2	K16
Cross Highway 20's Rainy Pass	R	0.9	2596.4	4855	1.8	K16
Porcupine Creek	w	1.5	2597.9	5080	1.6	L1
Cutthroat Pass	—	3.6	2601.5	6820	5.3	L1
Granite Pass	—	2.4	2603.9	6290	-2.4	L1
Large campsite	w	2.2	2606.1	6300	0.0	L2
Methow Pass	—	0.9	2607.0	6600	3.6	L2
Golden Creek and Willis Camp	w	4.2	2611.2	4570	-5.3	L2
West Fork Methow River	w	0.7	2611.9	4390	-2.8	L3
Merge with old Cascade Crest Trail (now Trail 756)	—	0.8	2612.7	4380	-0.1	L3
Junction with Mill Creek Trail 755	—	0.2	2612.9	4380	0.0	L3
West Fork Methow Trail 480, next to Brush Creek	w	1.9	2614.8	4280	-0.6	L3
Glacier Pass	—	2.8	2617.6	5520	4.8	L3
Alpine-garden pass above South Fork Trout Creek	—	2.6	2620.2	6750	5.1	L4
Pleasant trailside campsite with water	w	1.0	2621.2	6600	-1.6	L4
Windy, viewful pass on south-west shoulder of Tatie Peak	—	0.9	2622.1	6900	3.6	L4
20 yards before Road 500	R	2.8	2624.9	6440	-1.8	L4
Minor gap, see map for water source	w: 0.30m E	0.7	2625.6	6390	-0.8	L4
Water Alert (↓): 17.5m						
Harts Pass	—	1.3	2626.9	6198	-1.6	L4
Junction with a spur trail to a Forest Service road	R	1.4	2628.3	6880	5.3	L4

Washington

WASHINGTON

Landmark	Facilities	Diff	S->N	Elev	Gra	Map
Pass above Benson Creek Camp	—	2.2	2630.5	6700	-0.9	L5
Buffalo Pass	—	0.7	2631.2	6550	-2.3	L5
Windy Pass	—	0.9	2632.1	6257	-3.5	L5
Foggy Pass	—	2.2	2634.3	6180	-0.4	L5
Jim Pass	—	0.7	2635.0	6270	1.4	L5
Devils Backbone	—	1.3	2636.3	6180	-0.8	L6
Holman Pass	—	4.4	2640.7	5050	-2.8	L6
Spring and a good campsite	w	2.4	2643.1	6200	5.2	L6
Water Alert (↑): 17.8m						
Narrow crest pass Canyon Creek, alternate PCT route, south end	—	1.0	2644.1	6560	3.9	L6
Junction with alternate PCT route, north end	—	1.4	2645.5	6120	-3.4	L7
Junction with Trail 473	—	0.3	2645.8	6360	8.7	L7
Misnamed Woody Pass	—	0.5	2646.3	6624	5.7	L7
Faint trail to Mountain Home Camp	—	2.5	2648.8	6800	0.8	L7
Unnamed summit on Lakeview Ridge	—	0.7	2649.5	7126	5.1	L7
Spur trail to Hopkins Lake, campsites	w	1.7	2651.2	6220	-5.8	L7
Hopkins Pass	—	0.2	2651.4	6122	-5.3	L7
Castle Pass	w: 0.75m E	2.5	2653.9	5451	-2.9	L8
Monument 78, United States–Canada border, close to Castle Creek	—	4.1	2658.0	4240	-3.2	L9
Castle Creek	w	0.2	2658.2	4100	-7.6	L9
Southwest base of Windy Joe Mountain	—	3.5	2661.7	5070	3.0	L9
Junction with the Mt. Frosty Trail	w	0.3	2662.0	5120	1.8	L9

WASHINGTON

Landmark	Facilities	Diff	S->N	Elev	Gra	Map
Closed Windy Joe fire access road	R	0.7	2662.7	5220	1.6	L9
Junction with old PCT route	—	2.1	2664.8	4100	-5.8	L9
Trailhead parking area	R	1.3	2666.1	3980	-1.0	L9
Lightning Lake Campground 100% by reservations only (800) 689-9025	w,R: 2.00m W	0.0	2666.1	3800	-1.0	L9
Manning Park Resort (250) 840-8822	w 0.67m E; G 0.90m W; L 0.90m W;R	0.0	2666.1	3800	-1.0	L9
Manning Park Headquarters, BC, CANADA V0X 1R0	w 0.87m E; r 0.70m W;R	0.0	2666.1	3800	-1.0	L9
Coldspring Campground 50% by reservations (800) 689-9025, go towards Manning Park Resort first east, and then west	w,R: 1.90m NW	0.0	2666.1	3800	-1.0	L9

WASHINGTON

New Suiattle River Bridge Map

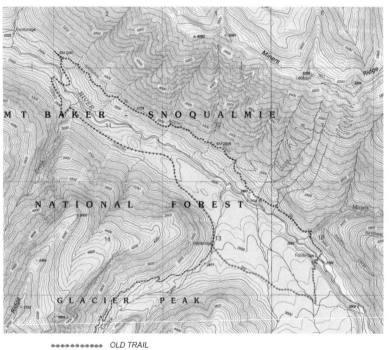

```
●●●●●●●●●●●  OLD TRAIL
++++++++++++  NEW TRAIL
```

Calendar

2014

January '14						
Su	M	Tu	W	Th	F	Sa
			1	2	3	4
5	6	7	8	9	10	11
12	13	14	15	16	17	18
19	20	21	22	23	24	25
26	27	28	29	30	31	

February '14						
Su	M	Tu	W	Th	F	Sa
						1
2	3	4	5	6	7	8
9	10	11	12	13	14	15
16	17	18	19	20	21	22
23	24	25	26	27	28	

March '14						
Su	M	Tu	W	Th	F	Sa
						1
2	3	4	5	6	7	8
9	10	11	12	13	14	15
16	17	18	19	20	21	22
23	24	25	26	27	28	29
30	31					

April '14						
Su	M	Tu	W	Th	F	Sa
		1	2	3	4	5
6	7	8	9	10	11	12
13	14	15	16	17	18	19
20	21	22	23	24	25	26
27	28	29	30			

May '14						
Su	M	Tu	W	Th	F	Sa
				1	2	3
4	5	6	7	8	9	10
11	12	13	14	15	16	17
18	19	20	21	22	23	24
25	26	27	28	29	30	31

June '14						
Su	M	Tu	W	Th	F	Sa
1	2	3	4	5	6	7
8	9	10	11	12	13	14
15	16	17	18	19	20	21
22	23	24	25	26	27	28
29	30					

July '14						
Su	M	Tu	W	Th	F	Sa
		1	2	3	4	5
6	7	8	9	10	11	12
13	14	15	16	17	18	19
20	21	22	23	24	25	26
27	28	29	30	31		

August '14						
Su	M	Tu	W	Th	F	Sa
					1	2
3	4	5	6	7	8	9
10	11	12	13	14	15	16
17	18	19	20	21	22	23
24	25	26	27	28	29	30
31						

September '14						
Su	M	Tu	W	Th	F	Sa
	1	2	3	4	5	6
7	8	9	10	11	12	13
14	15	16	17	18	19	20
21	22	23	24	25	26	27
28	29	30				

October '14						
Su	M	Tu	W	Th	F	Sa
			1	2	3	4
5	6	7	8	9	10	11
12	13	14	15	16	17	18
19	20	21	22	23	24	25
26	27	28	29	30	31	

November '14						
Su	M	Tu	W	Th	F	Sa
						1
2	3	4	5	6	7	8
9	10	11	12	13	14	15
16	17	18	19	20	21	22
23	24	25	26	27	28	29
30						

December '14						
Su	M	Tu	W	Th	F	Sa
	1	2	3	4	5	6
7	8	9	10	11	12	13
14	15	16	17	18	19	20
21	22	23	24	25	26	27
28	29	30	31			

Post Office Holidays

Jan 1, Jan 20, Feb 17, May 26, Jul 4,

Sep 1, Oct 13, Nov 11, Nov 27, Dec 25

2015

January '15

Su	M	Tu	W	Th	F	Sa
				1	2	3
4	5	6	7	8	9	10
11	12	13	14	15	16	17
18	19	20	21	22	23	24
25	26	27	28	29	30	31

February '15

Su	M	Tu	W	Th	F	Sa
1	2	3	4	5	6	7
8	9	10	11	12	13	14
15	16	17	18	19	20	21
22	23	24	25	26	27	28

March '15

Su	M	Tu	W	Th	F	Sa
1	2	3	4	5	6	7
8	9	10	11	12	13	14
15	16	17	18	19	20	21
22	23	24	25	26	27	28
29	30	31				

April '15

Su	M	Tu	W	Th	F	Sa
			1	2	3	4
5	6	7	8	9	10	11
12	13	14	15	16	17	18
19	20	21	22	23	24	25
26	27	28	29	30		

May '15

Su	M	Tu	W	Th	F	Sa
					1	2
3	4	5	6	7	8	9
10	11	12	13	14	15	16
17	18	19	20	21	22	23
24	25	26	27	28	29	30
31						

June '15

Su	M	Tu	W	Th	F	Sa
	1	2	3	4	5	6
7	8	9	10	11	12	13
14	15	16	17	18	19	20
21	22	23	24	25	26	27
28	29	30				

July '15

Su	M	Tu	W	Th	F	Sa
			1	2	3	4
5	6	7	8	9	10	11
12	13	14	15	16	17	18
19	20	21	22	23	24	25
26	27	28	29	30	31	

August '15

Su	M	Tu	W	Th	F	Sa
						1
2	3	4	5	6	7	8
9	10	11	12	13	14	15
16	17	18	19	20	21	22
23	24	25	26	27	28	29
30	31					

September '15

Su	M	Tu	W	Th	F	Sa
		1	2	3	4	5
6	7	8	9	10	11	12
13	14	15	16	17	18	19
20	21	22	23	24	25	26
27	28	29	30			

October '15

Su	M	Tu	W	Th	F	Sa
				1	2	3
4	5	6	7	8	9	10
11	12	13	14	15	16	17
18	19	20	21	22	23	24
25	26	27	28	29	30	31

November '15

Su	M	Tu	W	Th	F	Sa
1	2	3	4	5	6	7
8	9	10	11	12	13	14
15	16	17	18	19	20	21
22	23	24	25	26	27	28
29	30					

December '15

Su	M	Tu	W	Th	F	Sa
		1	2	3	4	5
6	7	8	9	10	11	12
13	14	15	16	17	18	19
20	21	22	23	24	25	26
27	28	29	30	31		

Post Office Holidays

Jan 1, Jan 19, Feb 16, May 25, Jul 3,

Sep 7, Oct 12, Nov 11, Nov 26, Dec 25

Calendar

2016

January '16

Su	M	Tu	W	Th	F	Sa
					1	2
3	4	5	6	7	8	9
10	11	12	13	14	15	16
17	18	19	20	21	22	23
24	25	26	27	28	29	30
31						

February '16

Su	M	Tu	W	Th	F	Sa
	1	2	3	4	5	6
7	8	9	10	11	12	13
14	15	16	17	18	19	20
21	22	23	24	25	26	27
28	29					

March '16

Su	M	Tu	W	Th	F	Sa
		1	2	3	4	5
6	7	8	9	10	11	12
13	14	15	16	17	18	19
20	21	22	23	24	25	26
27	28	29	30	31		

April '16

Su	M	Tu	W	Th	F	Sa
					1	2
3	4	5	6	7	8	9
10	11	12	13	14	15	16
17	18	19	20	21	22	23
24	25	26	27	28	29	30

May '16

Su	M	Tu	W	Th	F	Sa
1	2	3	4	5	6	7
8	9	10	11	12	13	14
15	16	17	18	19	20	21
22	23	24	25	26	27	28
29	30	31				

June '16

Su	M	Tu	W	Th	F	Sa
			1	2	3	4
5	6	7	8	9	10	11
12	13	14	15	16	17	18
19	20	21	22	23	24	25
26	27	28	29	30		

July '16

Su	M	Tu	W	Th	F	Sa
					1	2
3	4	5	6	7	8	9
10	11	12	13	14	15	16
17	18	19	20	21	22	23
24	25	26	27	28	29	30
31						

August '16

Su	M	Tu	W	Th	F	Sa
	1	2	3	4	5	6
7	8	9	10	11	12	13
14	15	16	17	18	19	20
21	22	23	24	25	26	27
28	29	30	31			

September '16

Su	M	Tu	W	Th	F	Sa
				1	2	3
4	5	6	7	8	9	10
11	12	13	14	15	16	17
18	19	20	21	22	23	24
25	26	27	28	29	30	

October '16

Su	M	Tu	W	Th	F	Sa
						1
2	3	4	5	6	7	8
9	10	11	12	13	14	15
16	17	18	19	20	21	22
23	24	25	26	27	28	29
30	31					

November '16

Su	M	Tu	W	Th	F	Sa
		1	2	3	4	5
6	7	8	9	10	11	12
13	14	15	16	17	18	19
20	21	22	23	24	25	26
27	28	29	30			

December '16

Su	M	Tu	W	Th	F	Sa
				1	2	3
4	5	6	7	8	9	10
11	12	13	14	15	16	17
18	19	20	21	22	23	24
25	26	27	28	29	30	31

Post Office Holidays

Jan 1, Jan 18, Feb 15, May 30, Jul 4,

Sep 5, Oct 10, Nov 11, Nov 24, Dec 26

Calendar

2017

January '17

Su	M	Tu	W	Th	F	Sa
1	2	3	4	5	6	7
8	9	10	11	12	13	14
15	16	17	18	19	20	21
22	23	24	25	26	27	28
29	30	31				

February '17

Su	M	Tu	W	Th	F	Sa
			1	2	3	4
5	6	7	8	9	10	11
12	13	14	15	16	17	18
19	20	21	22	23	24	25
26	27	28				

March '17

Su	M	Tu	W	Th	F	Sa
			1	2	3	4
5	6	7	8	9	10	11
12	13	14	15	16	17	18
19	20	21	22	23	24	25
26	27	28	29	30	31	

April '17

Su	M	Tu	W	Th	F	Sa
						1
2	3	4	5	6	7	8
9	10	11	12	13	14	15
16	17	18	19	20	21	22
23	24	25	26	27	28	29
30						

May '17

Su	M	Tu	W	Th	F	Sa
	1	2	3	4	5	6
7	8	9	10	11	12	13
14	15	16	17	18	19	20
21	22	23	24	25	26	27
28	29	30	31			

June '17

Su	M	Tu	W	Th	F	Sa
				1	2	3
4	5	6	7	8	9	10
11	12	13	14	15	16	17
18	19	20	21	22	23	24
25	26	27	28	29	30	

July '17

Su	M	Tu	W	Th	F	Sa
						1
2	3	4	5	6	7	8
9	10	11	12	13	14	15
16	17	18	19	20	21	22
23	24	25	26	27	28	29
30	31					

August '17

Su	M	Tu	W	Th	F	Sa
		1	2	3	4	5
6	7	8	9	10	11	12
13	14	15	16	17	18	19
20	21	22	23	24	25	26
27	28	29	30	31		

September '17

Su	M	Tu	W	Th	F	Sa
					1	2
3	4	5	6	7	8	9
10	11	12	13	14	15	16
17	18	19	20	21	22	23
24	25	26	27	28	29	30

October '17

Su	M	Tu	W	Th	F	Sa
1	2	3	4	5	6	7
8	9	10	11	12	13	14
15	16	17	18	19	20	21
22	23	24	25	26	27	28
29	30	31				

November '17

Su	M	Tu	W	Th	F	Sa
			1	2	3	4
5	6	7	8	9	10	11
12	13	14	15	16	17	18
19	20	21	22	23	24	25
26	27	28	29	30		

December '17

Su	M	Tu	W	Th	F	Sa
					1	2
3	4	5	6	7	8	9
10	11	12	13	14	15	16
17	18	19	20	21	22	23
24	25	26	27	28	29	30
31						

Post Office Holidays

Jan 2, Jan 16, Feb 20, May 29, Jul 4,

Sep 4, Oct 9, Nov 10, Nov 23, Dec 25

Calendar

2018

January '18
Su	M	Tu	W	Th	F	Sa
	1	2	3	4	5	6
7	8	9	10	11	12	13
14	15	16	17	18	19	20
21	22	23	24	25	26	27
28	29	30	31			

February '18
Su	M	Tu	W	Th	F	Sa
				1	2	3
4	5	6	7	8	9	10
11	12	13	14	15	16	17
18	19	20	21	22	23	24
25	26	27	28			

March '18
Su	M	Tu	W	Th	F	Sa
				1	2	3
4	5	6	7	8	9	10
11	12	13	14	15	16	17
18	19	20	21	22	23	24
25	26	27	28	29	30	31

April '18
Su	M	Tu	W	Th	F	Sa
1	2	3	4	5	6	7
8	9	10	11	12	13	14
15	16	17	18	19	20	21
22	23	24	25	26	27	28
29	30					

May '18
Su	M	Tu	W	Th	F	Sa
		1	2	3	4	5
6	7	8	9	10	11	12
13	14	15	16	17	18	19
20	21	22	23	24	25	26
27	28	29	30	31		

June '18
Su	M	Tu	W	Th	F	Sa
					1	2
3	4	5	6	7	8	9
10	11	12	13	14	15	16
17	18	19	20	21	22	23
24	25	26	27	28	29	30

July '18
Su	M	Tu	W	Th	F	Sa
1	2	3	4	5	6	7
8	9	10	11	12	13	14
15	16	17	18	19	20	21
22	23	24	25	26	27	28
29	30	31				

August '18
Su	M	Tu	W	Th	F	Sa
			1	2	3	4
5	6	7	8	9	10	11
12	13	14	15	16	17	18
19	20	21	22	23	24	25
26	27	28	29	30	31	

September '18
Su	M	Tu	W	Th	F	Sa
						1
2	3	4	5	6	7	8
9	10	11	12	13	14	15
16	17	18	19	20	21	22
23	24	25	26	27	28	29
30						

October '18
Su	M	Tu	W	Th	F	Sa
	1	2	3	4	5	6
7	8	9	10	11	12	13
14	15	16	17	18	19	20
21	22	23	24	25	26	27
28	29	30	31			

November '18
Su	M	Tu	W	Th	F	Sa
				1	2	3
4	5	6	7	8	9	10
11	12	13	14	15	16	17
18	19	20	21	22	23	24
25	26	27	28	29	30	

December '18
Su	M	Tu	W	Th	F	Sa
						1
2	3	4	5	6	7	8
9	10	11	12	13	14	15
16	17	18	19	20	21	22
23	24	25	26	27	28	29
30	31					

Post Office Holidays

Jan 1, Jan 15, Feb 19, May 28, Jul 4,

Sep 3, Oct 8, Nov 12, Nov 22, Dec 25

Calendar

2019

January '19
Su	M	Tu	W	Th	F	Sa
		1	2	3	4	5
6	7	8	9	10	11	12
13	14	15	16	17	18	19
20	21	22	23	24	25	26
27	28	29	30	31		

February '19
Su	M	Tu	W	Th	F	Sa
					1	2
3	4	5	6	7	8	9
10	11	12	13	14	15	16
17	18	19	20	21	22	23
24	25	26	27	28		

March '19
Su	M	Tu	W	Th	F	Sa
					1	2
3	4	5	6	7	8	9
10	11	12	13	14	15	16
17	18	19	20	21	22	23
24	25	26	27	28	29	30
31						

April '19
Su	M	Tu	W	Th	F	Sa
	1	2	3	4	5	6
7	8	9	10	11	12	13
14	15	16	17	18	19	20
21	22	23	24	25	26	27
28	29	30				

May '19
Su	M	Tu	W	Th	F	Sa
			1	2	3	4
5	6	7	8	9	10	11
12	13	14	15	16	17	18
19	20	21	22	23	24	25
26	27	28	29	30	31	

June '19
Su	M	Tu	W	Th	F	Sa
						1
2	3	4	5	6	7	8
9	10	11	12	13	14	15
16	17	18	19	20	21	22
23	24	25	26	27	28	29
30						

July '19
Su	M	Tu	W	Th	F	Sa
	1	2	3	4	5	6
7	8	9	10	11	12	13
14	15	16	17	18	19	20
21	22	23	24	25	26	27
28	29	30	31			

August '19
Su	M	Tu	W	Th	F	Sa
				1	2	3
4	5	6	7	8	9	10
11	12	13	14	15	16	17
18	19	20	21	22	23	24
25	26	27	28	29	30	31

September '19
Su	M	Tu	W	Th	F	Sa
1	2	3	4	5	6	7
8	9	10	11	12	13	14
15	16	17	18	19	20	21
22	23	24	25	26	27	28
29	30					

October '19
Su	M	Tu	W	Th	F	Sa
		1	2	3	4	5
6	7	8	9	10	11	12
13	14	15	16	17	18	19
20	21	22	23	24	25	26
27	28	29	30	31		

November '19
Su	M	Tu	W	Th	F	Sa
					1	2
3	4	5	6	7	8	9
10	11	12	13	14	15	16
17	18	19	20	21	22	23
24	25	26	27	28	29	30

December '19
Su	M	Tu	W	Th	F	Sa
1	2	3	4	5	6	7
8	9	10	11	12	13	14
15	16	17	18	19	20	21
22	23	24	25	26	27	28
29	30	31				

Post Office Holidays

Jan 1, Jan 21, Feb 18, May 27, Jul 4,

Sep 2, Oct 14, Nov 11, Nov 28, Dec 25

Calendar

2020

January '20

Su	M	Tu	W	Th	F	Sa
			1	2	3	4
5	6	7	8	9	10	11
12	13	14	15	16	17	18
19	20	21	22	23	24	25
26	27	28	29	30	31	

February '20

Su	M	Tu	W	Th	F	Sa
						1
2	3	4	5	6	7	8
9	10	11	12	13	14	15
16	17	18	19	20	21	22
23	24	25	26	27	28	29

March '20

Su	M	Tu	W	Th	F	Sa
1	2	3	4	5	6	7
8	9	10	11	12	13	14
15	16	17	18	19	20	21
22	23	24	25	26	27	28
29	30	31				

April '20

Su	M	Tu	W	Th	F	Sa
			1	2	3	4
5	6	7	8	9	10	11
12	13	14	15	16	17	18
19	20	21	22	23	24	25
26	27	28	29	30		

May '20

Su	M	Tu	W	Th	F	Sa
					1	2
3	4	5	6	7	8	9
10	11	12	13	14	15	16
17	18	19	20	21	22	23
24	25	26	27	28	29	30
31						

June '20

Su	M	Tu	W	Th	F	Sa
	1	2	3	4	5	6
7	8	9	10	11	12	13
14	15	16	17	18	19	20
21	22	23	24	25	26	27
28	29	30				

July '20

Su	M	Tu	W	Th	F	Sa
			1	2	3	4
5	6	7	8	9	10	11
12	13	14	15	16	17	18
19	20	21	22	23	24	25
26	27	28	29	30	31	

August '20

Su	M	Tu	W	Th	F	Sa
						1
2	3	4	5	6	7	8
9	10	11	12	13	14	15
16	17	18	19	20	21	22
23	24	25	26	27	28	29
30	31					

September '20

Su	M	Tu	W	Th	F	Sa
		1	2	3	4	5
6	7	8	9	10	11	12
13	14	15	16	17	18	19
20	21	22	23	24	25	26
27	28	29	30			

October '20

Su	M	Tu	W	Th	F	Sa
				1	2	3
4	5	6	7	8	9	10
11	12	13	14	15	16	17
18	19	20	21	22	23	24
25	26	27	28	29	30	31

November '20

Su	M	Tu	W	Th	F	Sa
1	2	3	4	5	6	7
8	9	10	11	12	13	14
15	16	17	18	19	20	21
22	23	24	25	26	27	28
29	30					

December '20

Su	M	Tu	W	Th	F	Sa
		1	2	3	4	5
6	7	8	9	10	11	12
13	14	15	16	17	18	19
20	21	22	23	24	25	26
27	28	29	30	31		

Post Office Holidays

Jan 1, Jan 20, Feb 17, May 25, Jul 3,

Sep 7, Oct 12, Nov 11, Nov 26, Dec 25

Contacts

Name:

Address:

City, State, Zip:

Phone:

Email:

Name:

Address:

City, State, Zip:

Phone:

Email:

Name:

Address:

City, State, Zip:

Phone:

Email:

Name:

Address:

City, State, Zip:

Phone:

Email:

Name:

Address:

City, State, Zip:

Phone:

Email:

Contacts

Name:

Address:

City, State, Zip:

Phone:

Email:

Name:

Address:

City, State, Zip:

Phone:

Email:

Name:

Address:

City, State, Zip:

Phone:

Email:

Name:

Address:

City, State, Zip:

Phone:

Email:

Name:

Address:

City, State, Zip:

Phone:

Email:

Pacific Crest Trail Association

A VOICE FOR THE TRAIL

PACIFIC CREST TRAIL
A S S O C I A T I O N

The Pacific Crest Trail Association (PCTA) is an effective advocate for the protection and wise management of the Pacific Crest National Scenic Trail. Through our member magazine, publications, toll-free telephone number, and website, the PCTA reports route changes, pending legislation, trail conditions, and activities that might threaten the largely pristine trail corridor.

Without constant attention, the trail would quickly succumb to the effects of humans and the forces of nature. Working in partnership with the USDA Forest Service, the National Park Service, the Bureau of Land Management, as well as state and private landowners, the PCTA organizes volunteer crews to help preserve the trail. Members also gather and report trail conditions, which are relayed to appropriate officials.

The PCTA encourages good trail ethics, no-trace camping, and an awareness of the Pacific Crest National Scenic Trail as a valued national heritage.

The mission of the Pacific Crest Trail Association is to protect, preserve and promote the Pacific Crest National Scenic Trail so as to reflect its world-class significance for the enjoyment, education and adventure of hikers and equestrians.

The PCTA is a 501(c)(3) tax-exempt nonprofit organization. Your membership and donations are critical in keeping this national treasure alive. Join us!

Pacific Crest Trail Association

MEMBERSHIP BENEFITS

Help Preserve the Pacific Crest National Scenic Trail. As a member of the PCTA, you can help protect, preserve, and promote the Pacific Crest National Scenic Trail for this generation and all that follow. Join us!

- ☐ $35 Trail Guide
- ☐ $50 Trail Advocate
- ☐ $1000 Trail Guardian
- ☐ $100 Trail Partner
- ☐ $500 Trail Builder
- ☐ $25 Trail Explorer (Senior/Student)

All members will receive:

- The knowledge that their membership helps to protect and preserve the PCT for future generations
- The PCTA magazine, *PCTA Communicator*
- A one-year subscription to *Backpacker* magazine (US only)
- A Pacific Crest Trail decal
- Discounts on PCTA store items and PCTA activities
- Invitations to participate in trail classes and volunteer trail projects

Donate and join PCTA online at **www.pcta.org/donate.**

Pacific Crest Trail Association

JANE AND FLICKA ENDOWMENT FUND

All the proceeds of this book will be donated by the author to the Jane and Flicka Endowment Fund. Jane and Flicka were two hikers who lost their lives on a thru-hike of the PCT when a car struck them on the highway near the end of their journey. They were returning to the trail after a stop in a nearby town for supplies.

Family and friends established this Endowment Fund in their memory to benefit the PCTA and to keep their spirit alive along the trail. This fund is used to maintain the Pacific Crest National Scenic Trail and promote its use by individuals from around the world.

A message from Barbara Perry, Flicka's mother:

> "I have walked the highway where Jane and Flicka died. We considered putting a memorial up for them, to join the others, yet we did not want to remember or memorialize that place. We wanted to think of them out on the trail, in God's country, and so we chose their memorial to be the Jane and Flicka Endowment Fund for the PCTA—something that will live forever and help to preserve the trail for others to be inspired.
>
> Flicka and Jane always knew, way beyond their years, exactly how precious life is, which is one reason they touched so many in their lives and their death. In Flicka's last journal were words from Thoreau: 'I went to the woods because I wished to live deliberately, to front only the essential facts of life, and see if I could not learn what it had to teach, and not, when I came to die, discover that I had not lived. Living is so dear . . .'
>
> The Jane and Flicka Endowment Fund was created to help preserve and protect the trail by providing a foundation for the PCTA. The spirit of Jane and Flicka continues to inspire all of us in ways great and small."

If you would like to contribute to the Fund, please send donations to the PCTA, referencing "Jane and Flicka Endowment Fund" on the check.

ぼくの 最愛の もの、
これが 全部 夢 ならば、
ああ、目覚めたくはなし。

My Beloved,
If this is all a dream,
Then, I do not want to wake up.

Authoritative Guidebooks
to the Entire PCT

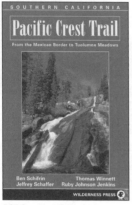
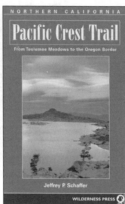
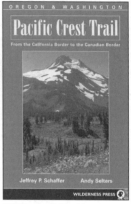

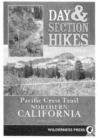

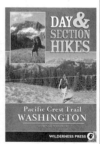